• A HISTORY LOVER'S •
GUIDE TO

LOUISVILLE

A HISTORY LOVER'S
GUIDE TO
LOUISVILLE

BRYAN S. BUSH

THE
History
PRESS

Published by The History Press
Charleston, SC
www.historypress.com

Front cover, top left: Courtesy of Samantha Del Pozo, CTA. The Brown Hotel, associate director of sales; *top center*: courtesy of Steve Wiser; *top right*: courtesy of Steve Wiser; *bottom*: Courtesy of Christian Adelberg, vice-president, marketing and communication, Kentucky Performing Arts.
Back cover: courtesy of Steve Wiser; *inset*: courtesy of Steve Wiser.

First published 2021

Manufactured in the United States

ISBN 9781467148689

Library of Congress Control Number: 2020951665

CONTENTS

ACKNOWLEDGEMENTS

Special thanks must go to the Seelbach Hotel, the Brown Hotel, the Kentucky Center for the Arts, the American Printing House for the Blind, Cave Hill Cemetery, the University of Louisville Digital Archives, the Louisville Free Public Library and The History Press. My parents, Carol Bush and Gene Bush, and my stepmom, Joan Bush.

Many of the photographs in the book were provided by Steve Wiser. Steve is a Louisville architect, historian and author. For over thirty-five years, he has specialized in healthcare facility planning, design and construction. He has built over $2 billion in healthcare projects and designed every type of healthcare project: critical access hospitals, academic medical centers, for-profit/nonprofit institutions, patient units, cancer centers, behavioral health centers and clinics, among others. He is president of the Louisville Historical League. Steve is also a tour guide at Cave Hill Cemetery and conducts neighborhood walking tours. He has written over ten books on Louisville architecture and history. Steve received his architectural training at the University of Cincinnati.

INTRODUCTION

In Louisville's 240-year history, the city has gone through many changes and encountered difficult times, but despite those hard times, Louisville has always come out strong and vibrant. Louisville started as a small settlement of families on Corn Island, led by General George Rogers Clark. Today, it is the largest city in Kentucky and the twenty-ninth-largest city in the country.

Because of the Falls of the Ohio, Louisville quickly grew from a small settlement on Corn Island to one that moved to the Ohio River shore. By 1781, the thriving community had built Fort Nelson. By April 1792, the Commonwealth of Kentucky became the fifteenth state admitted to the United States. At the time, Louisville had two hundred houses. When Kentucky became a state, new settlers flowed in through the Cumberland Gap on the Wilderness Road. In 1803, Meriwether Lewis and William Clark met in Louisville to form one of the most famous and successful partnerships in history. The Corps of Discovery set off from Clarksville, Indiana, and journeyed to the Pacific Ocean, after which it headed back to Kentucky. In 1807, John James Audubon, the naturalist, ornithologist and painter, came down the Ohio River from Pittsburg, Pennsylvania, and set up a general store with Jean Ferdinand Rozier. Audubon lived in the city for ten years.

In 1811, Robert Fulton built the *Orleans* steamboat in Pittsburg; in October of that year, it undertook its maiden voyage down the Ohio River. The *Orleans* was the start of the steamboat industry, which the Louisville economy relied on and which made the city profitable. By 1820, Louisville was a thriving and prosperous little town, with 670 buildings; of these, 65 were licensed stores and the remainder were small shops and homes. There were 38 doctors and the same number of lawyers, 4 ropewalks, 15 brickyards and quite a number of manufactories. During the 1830s through the 1850s, Louisville became a major steamboat city. Across the river in Jeffersonville, with the Howard Shipyards and New Albany's six shipyards, hundreds of steamboats were built. Agricultural goods from the Midwest and Kentucky were shipped to New Orleans and other ports along the Ohio and Mississippi Rivers. One of the major factors that allowed steamboat traffic was the Portland Canal. On January 12, 1825, the Louisville and Portland Canal Company was incorporated by the legislature, and work began in March 1826. In 1830, at a cost of $750,000, the canal was completed and opened to navigation. Today, the Portland Canal, which is now the McAlpine Locks and Dam, continues in operation.

In 1850, Louisville became the tenth-largest city in the United States. Its population rose from 10,000 in 1830 to 43,000 in 1850. Louisville became an important tobacco market and pork-packing center. By 1850, Louisville's wholesale trade totaled $20 million in sales. The Louisville–New Orleans river route held top rank in the entire western river system in freight and passenger traffic. Not only did Louisville profit from the river, but also, in August 1855, Louisville citizens greeted the arrival of the locomotive *Hart County* on Ninth and Broadway. Hemp was Kentucky's leading agricultural product from 1840 to 1860, and Louisville was the nation's leading hemp market.

During the 1850s, Louisville became a prosperous city, but by 1860, war loomed over the American landscape. In April 1861, the country went to war. An important state geographically, Kentucky had the Ohio River as a natural barrier. Kentucky's natural resources, manpower and the Louisville and Nashville Railroad (L&N) made both the North and South respect the state's neutrality. U.S. president Abraham Lincoln and Confederate president Jefferson Davis kept a hands-off policy when dealing with Kentucky, hoping not to the push the state into one camp or the other. The L&N's depot on Ninth and Broadway and the steamboats at Louisville's wharfs sent uniforms, lead, bacon, coffee and war material south. Lincoln did not want to stop the city from sending goods south, for the fear of upsetting Kentucky's delicate balance of neutrality. But on July 10, 1861, a federal judge in Louisville ruled that the U.S. government had the right to stop shipments of goods going south over the L&N. Once neutrality had been broken in the state by September 1861, Louisville became a staging ground for Union troops heading south. Troops flowed into Louisville from Ohio, Indiana, Pennsylvania and Wisconsin. White tents and training grounds sprang up at the Oakland track, Old Louisville and Portland. Camps were also established at Eighteenth and Broadway, along the Frankfort and Bardstown Turnpikes.

By early 1862, Louisville had eighty thousand Union troops throughout the city. With so many troops, entrepreneurs set up gambling establishments along the north side of Jefferson from Fourth to Fifth Streets, around the corner on Fifth Street to Market and on the south side of Market Street back to Fourth Street. Photography studios and military goods shops, such as Fletcher & Bennett on Main Street and Hirschbuhl & Sons on Main Street, east of Third Street, catered to the Union officers and soldiers. With so many troops, brothels also sprang up around the city. The Louisville and Nashville Railroad and the steamboats in Louisville transported troops deeper into the South.

After the Battle of Perryville, Kentucky, on October 8, 1862, the massive amount of wounded flooded into Louisville. Hospitals were set up in public schools, homes, factories and churches. The Fifth Ward School, built at Fifth and York Streets in 1855, became Military Hospital Number Eight. The United States Marine Hospital also became a hospital for wounded Union soldiers from the battle. Constructed between 1845 and 1852, the three-story Greek Revival–style Louisville Marine Hospital contained one hundred beds and became the prototype for seven U.S. Marine Hospital Service buildings, including at Paducah, Kentucky, which later became Fort Anderson. Union surgeons erected the Brown General Hospital, located near the Belnap campus of the University of Louisville, and other hospitals were built at Jeffersonville and New Albany, Indiana. By early 1863, the War Department and the U.S. Sanitary Commission had erected nineteen hospitals. By early June 1863, 930 deaths had been recorded in the Louisville hospitals, and Cave Hill Cemetery set aside plots for the Union dead.

After the Civil War, Louisville resumed becoming an industrial city. Union general Jeremiah Boyle returned to the city to start the new Louisville City Railway. Plans were made to rebuild the Galt House on First and Main Streets. The Robert Rowell Electrotype Company was established, which was the first foundry south of the Ohio River. Josiah B. Garthright, a first lieutenant in General John Hunt Morgan's cavalry, built the saddle firm Gathright and Company.

The end of the Civil War opened up the southern states to the markets along the border, and Louisville became the center of trade and commerce. Trade and industry had a vigorous and successful start, and the growth of the city led to prosperity. Among the contributing factors in Louisville becoming an industrial city were the following: the establishment of new railroads and the extension of old ones; the bridging of the Ohio River; the improvement of the Portland Canal and of river navigation; the introduction of modern methods in every sector of business life; and the erection of buildings devoted to commerce, manufacturing and domestic purposes. After the war, ex-slaves and their families flocked to Louisville and helped provide a ready source of manpower. Foreign immigrants found opportunities in the new industrial city. Former Confederate soldiers took advantage of the opportunities in the thriving commerce center, which was undamaged by the war.

During the Gilded Age, railroads helped the city become prosperous again. By 1885, the L&N had control of 2,027 miles of track and transported 569,149 people. In 1875, Churchill Downs was founded. Two of the leading industries in Louisville during the Gilded Age were whiskey and tobacco. Louisville was the largest market in the United States and the largest market in the world for jeans and jeans clothing. It was also the largest manufacturer of cast-iron gas and water pipes in the United States, made by the firm Dennis Long & Company, of the Union Pipe Works. Louisville led the world in farm wagons. Louisville was also the largest manufacturer of plows in the world. It led the world in hydraulic cement; most of the cement was made largely from the mills operating on the cement stone in the bed of the Ohio River. Louisville led the world in the manufacture of tanned sole and harness leather.

In 1917, during World War I, the War Department built Camp Zachary Taylor. Also during 1917–18, the Spanish flu epidemic raged through Camp Zachary Taylor and Louisville.

By January 24, 1937, 40 percent of residential Louisville was underwater. All light and power failed, but Louisville rebuilt. In 1940, during World War II, the U.S. Naval Ordnance Plant was built adjacent to the Louisville and Nashville Railroad at Strawberry Yards. Built by the federal government, it was operated by Westinghouse Electric and Manufacturing Company.

During the 1950s, the Black population rose from 47,200 in 1940 to 57,800. Republican Eugene S. Clayton became the first African American to serve as alderman. In the postwar period, Blacks fought for equality. In 1948, the Louisville Free Public Library opened its facility to African Americans. In 1950, the Kentucky General Assembly repealed the Day Law, which was an act to prohibit White and Black people from attending the same school.

In the 1960s and '70s, downtown Louisville began to decline as a result of suburban growth. With urban renewal, old landmarks and buildings were torn down. A preservation movement began with the Old Louisville Association. In the 1980s, downtown Louisville began the city's revitalization. In 1982, the Auchter Company began construction on the Humana Tower. In 1983, the Kentucky Center for the Arts opened. Ten years later, the AEGON Center was completed, which became Louisville's tallest building.

In 1999, Phase I of the Louisville Waterfront Park was completed; in 2004, Phase II was completed. In 2014, the Big Four Bridge was converted into a bicycle and pedestrian bridge. In 2000, Louisville Slugger Field opened for the newly renamed Louisville Bats, which became the minor-league affiliate for the Cincinnati Reds. In 2004, Frazier International History Museum opened to the public. On November 19, 2005, the Muhammed Ali Center opened as a nonprofit museum and cultural center in Louisville. On October 10, 2010, the KFC Yum! Center opened to the public. In 2020, the U.S. Lynn Family Stadium opened. It hosts the Louisville City FC soccer team and will become the home to Racing Louisville FC of the National Women's Soccer League in 2021.

As the COVID-19 virus rages throughout the country, its effect on Louisville and the city's progress remains to be seen. But if anything has been learned from Louisville's 240-year past, the city will recover. One can only hope that the city will bounce back and continue to be the "Bourbon City" and that the Kentucky Derby, the Kentucky Hot Brown at the Brown Hotel, the Seelbach, the Frazier Museum, the Louisville Science Center, the *Belle of Louisville*, the Galt House and many other Louisville historic sites and traditions will weather the storm and come out even stronger.

Chapter 1

CORN ISLAND AND GEORGE ROGERS CLARK

On June 2, 1765, Colonel George Croghan, an Indian trader employed by the British government, made his way down the Ohio River from Pittsburgh, Pennsylvania, and wrote a note in his diary that he had embarked and passed the Falls of the Ohio. The river was low at the time, and his men had to lighten their boats and pass on the north side of a little island located in the middle of the river.[1]

In 1766, British captains Harry Gordon and Thomas Hutchins, of the Sixteenth Regiment Foot of the British Service, camped at the Falls of the Ohio and drew a map of the mouth of Beargrass Creek, which was a natural harbor rising through eight springs that verged into the main body of the stream and for the last half mile ran parallel to the Ohio River. The map was published in London in 1778. Hutchins drew a portion of the Ohio River six miles long from Sandy Island to one mile above the foot of Beargrass Creek. In his map, he drew Corn Island, Rock Island, Sandy Island and Goose Island. In 1772 and 1774, he surveyed the surrounding country. Hutchins died in 1789 in Pittsburgh.[2] In 1773, William and Mary College in Virginia gave a special commission to Captain Thomas Bullitt to survey lands and influence settlements in the territory of Kentucky. On July 8, 1773, he and a small company landed at the mouth of Beargrass Creek at the Falls of the Ohio and established a camp. He made surveys as far as the Salt River. Before he completed his survey, he laid out a town site comprising part of Louisville, which he called the "Falls of the Ohio."[3]

In December 1773, John Connolly owned two thousand acres of land, given to him for his service in the French and Indian Wars. Captain Thomas Bullitt surveyed the lands at the Falls for Connolly and others. In August 1773, Bullitt laid out a town on the land he had surveyed. He was the first man known to have selected the Falls for the site of a town. In August of that year, Colonel John Campbell contracted Connolly for half of his land at the Falls and became interested in Louisville. In April 1774, Connolly and Campbell jointly issued proposals for the sale of lots in a town to be established at the Falls of the Ohio. Before the lots could be sold to settlers and homes built, in October 1774, Connolly had trouble at Fort Pitt, in Pennsylvania, which led to a battle with Native Americans at Point Pleasant. The Native Americans lost the battle and asked for peace. A treaty was signed. During the American Revolution, Connolly sided with the British and, while attempting to organize a regiment of Native Americans to lead against the colonists in 1775, was arrested by the colonists and imprisoned. In 1779, Campbell, who decided to support the colonists, was also taken prisoner by the Native Americans while traveling from Louisville to Pittsburgh on one of Captain David Rogers's boats. Both Connolly and Campbell were prisoners and not able to settle the Falls.[4]

In 1776, Captain William Linn set out from Pittsburgh on a boat headed to New Orleans with war material to be used by the colonists against England. The boat reached New Orleans, where he secured his cargo. On his return trip, he reached the Falls of the Ohio in the spring of 1777. At the foot of the Falls with 150 kegs of black powder, Linn took the kegs off his boat and carried them around the Falls and put them back on the boat above the Falls. Linn took his boat on to Pittsburgh, where the powder was used by the colonists against England.

On January 22, 1778, the Virginia Council in Williamsburg authorized Colonel George Rogers Clark to enlist seven companies to "go to Kentucke." The council instructed Clark to proceed "with all convenient speed, to raise seven companies of soldiers, to consist of fifty men each, officered in the usual manner and armed most properly for the enterprise; and with this force attack the British post at Kaskaskia."[5] The order stated that there were several pieces of artillery and military stores at the fort and once taken by Clark would become a valuable asset for Virginia. The order was signed by Governor Patrick Henry.

In early May 1778, George Rogers Clark left Redstone, on the Monongahela River, with 150 men on a secret mission to conquer the British posts in the Illinois country. Against his will, he also took twenty families

The General George Rogers Clark statue was sculpted by Felix W. de Weldon in 1970. Arthur E. Hopkins donated the statue to Louisville. It is located on the riverfront plaza behind the Kentucky Theater Center for the Arts.

George Rogers Clark statue, located at Belvedere. *Courtesy of Steve Wiser.*

with him who had plans to settle in Kentucky. His flotilla comprised ten vessels. On May 27, Clark and his party landed on Corn Island. Clark was the first White man to step foot on the island. Native American hunters had dropped corn kernels when they camped on the island in the past, and corn grew on the island naturally. Clark landed on Corn Island for the purpose of turning his raw recruits into soldiers, and knew that the recruits could not escape the island. He feared that if he told his untrained militia recruits his plans to lead them against the Native Americans of the Illinois country, some of them might desert. Clark gave names to three other islands nearby, calling them Goose, Rock and Sandy. James Chenoweth, who was a member of the party, tore apart the rafts and used the lumber to build log cabins. Corn Island was cleared, and a stockade was built. The families built eighteen cabins, six of them blockhouses, with twelve families living in the cabins. Some of the names that were recorded of the families that stayed in the fort were the following: James Patton and his wife, Mary, and their three daughters, Martha, Peggy and Mary; Richard and Margaret Chenoweth and their four children, Mildred, Jane, James and Thomas; John McManness and his wife, Mary, and their three children, John, George and James; William and Elizabeth Faith and their son, John; John Tewell and his wife, Mary, and their three children, Ann, Winnie and Jessie; Jacob and Elizabeth Reager and their three children, Sarah, Mariah and Henry; Edward Worthington and his wife, Mary, his son, Charles, and Edward's two sisters, Mary (Mrs. James Graham) and Elizabeth (Mrs. Jacob Reager); James and Mary Graham; John and Martha Donne, their son, John, and their African American slave, Cato Watts;, Isaac Kimberly and his wife, Mary; Joseph Hunter and his children, Joseph, David, James, Martha and Ann; Neal Dougherty; Samuel Perkins; John Sinclair; and Robert Travis. The fort became the first permanent settlement of Louisville.[6]

On June 24, Clark and 150 men set off on their secret mission, leaving a small band of settlers on Corn Island. Clark and his men captured three important British forts at Kaskaskia and Cahokia on the Mississippi River near St. Louis and Vincennes on the Wabash River. By July 1778, Clark had conquered the Illinois country. From directions given by Clark, the inhabitants of Corn Island left the island and built a fort on the east side of a ravine that entered the Ohio River, on present-day Twelfth Street. Richard Chenoweth was the architect of the new fort. It was designed as a parallelogram, two hundred feet long by one hundred feet wide, consisting of eight single-story double cabins on each of the two long sides and four on each of the two short sides. At each of the four corners were blockhouses two stories high and twenty-four feet square. On December 25, 1778, the inhabitants completed the new fort by the shore.

By 1779, there were 150 soldiers camped at the Falls of the Ohio, and they had set up seven stations. Settlers arrived every week at the Falls, and plans were made to build cabins outside the fort. A bridge was built across Beargrass Creek. The Kentucky County Court sent instructions to the various stations for laying out new towns. John Corbly drew a plan showing eighty-eight half-acre plots on two sides of a street and twenty-eight additional lots near the northern bend of the Ohio River. George Rogers Clark wrote to the settlement at Corn Island that the city should be named after Louis XVI of France, who was giving the United States aid against Great Britain, and call the city Louisville. A new town was drawn, and already three of the streets were named: Main, Market and Jefferson. The cross streets were numbered First through Twelfth.[7]

Chapter 2

LOUISVILLE BECOMES A CITY

O n May 1, 1780, the Virginia legislature passed an act for the establishment of the town of Louisville at the Falls of the Ohio. A one-story log courthouse was built, and on March 7, 1781, there was a meeting of the justices of the peace of Louisville and the first court of the county was held in the fort. Kentucky County was in the state of Virginia and divided into Fayette, Lincoln and Jefferson Counties. The governor of Virginia appointed Richard Chenoweth as sheriff of the county. Brigadier General George Rogers Clark returned from his victorious conquest of the Illinois country to settle in Louisville. In 1781, he ordered the building of a larger and stronger fort, which was located on Main Street between Sixth and Eighth Streets and named after Virginia governor Thomas Nelson Jr. General Clark brought a six-pound cannon he had captured from Vincennes for the fort.[8]

Fort Nelson Park
West Main Street and South Seventh Streets

The park is located in Louisville in a small corner park plaza with shade trees and a fountain in the center. The history of the small park dates to 1991, when the landscape and urban design firm EDAW, now part of architecture and engineering giant AECOM, was commissioned by the Louisville Development Authority to design a

This page: Captain Richard Chenoweth, buried in Long Run Cemetery, Jefferson County. *Courtesy of the author.*

streetscape along West Main Street that fit in to the area's unique history and cast-iron architecture. Part of the streetscape project included a $350,000 pocket park replacing an earlier 1960s park rumored to have been designed by the successor firms of Frederick Law Olmsted. The old Colonial Dames monument, a rough-hewn stone obelisk created in 1912, had a plague that reads: "To commemorate the establishment of the town of Louisville, 1780. On this site stood Fort Nelson, built 1782 under the direction of George Rogers Clark after the expedition which gave to the country the Great Northwest." The monument stands prominently at the corner. Fort Nelson Park has a design based on a formal Victorian sitting park. The park incorporated remnants of demolished cast-iron buildings to form gateways into the park. Fort Nelson Park also had a cast-iron fountain salvaged from the Southern Exposition. The fountain was from the 1870s estate, which was located in Central Park and built by Reverend Stuart Robinson and later owned by Bidermann DuPont. There were originally four fountains at each corner of the Southern Exposition building. In October 2014, the fountain was removed from Fort Nelson Park and put into storage, where it remains.[9]

This page and opposite: Fort Nelson Park, 700 West Main Street. *Courtesy of the author.*

Fort Nelson Building
Eighth and Main Streets

The Fort Nelson Building dates to the 1890s, and the building was named after the very first fort that protected Louisville and served many uses, including the Abraham Hat Company. The building is currently the Michter's Fort Nelson Distillery. The company spent millions of dollars renovating the building. Michter is America's oldest bourbon company, founded in 1753. The distillery opened its doors in 2019.

In 1791, James and Mary Patton build the first stone house in Louisville. An observatory was built on the roof, used to keep an eye out for approaching river craft. His house was located on the northeast corner of Eighth and Main Streets. Squire Boone, brother of the famous American pioneer Daniel Boone, built a house from the boards of a flatboat, but the wood was wet, and when the boards dried, they shrank and warped. So Boone abandoned his home in Louisville and left for his fort at present-day Shelbyville. He eventually built his own station. In 1788, Michael Lacassagne, a Frenchman who was the first postmaster for Louisville, built a French cottage. He was also a merchant in the city. In 1789, Augustus Kaye built the first brick house in the city. The bricks had been manufactured in Pittsburgh and brought to Louisville on flatboats. In 1887, Alexander Scott Bullitt, a nephew of Captain Thomas Bullitt, settled about nine miles from town on a thousand-acre tract of land bordering Beargrass Creek. He named his farm Oxmoor, from the book *Tristram Shandy*, and built a large log cabin. The house has been continually improved and has become one of the handsomest estates in Jefferson County.

In 1782, Barthelemi Tardiveau and Honore, two French citizens who had settled near Shippingport, known as Campbelltown, undertook the first commercial trip by boat from Louisville to New Orleans. Their trip was the beginning of the great river trade that was the foundation on which the prosperity of Louisville relied.

In 1783, Daniel Brodhead built the first real store on the north side of Main Street, between Fifth and Sixth. He brought his goods on wagon over the mountains from Philadelphia. He sold glass window lights and calico and chip straw bonnets. Michael Humble set up a gunsmith shop on Twelfth between Main; next door was William Spangler, who established

Michter's Distillery in the Fort Nelson Building. *Courtesy of Steve Wiser.*

a forge shop for making farm implements and shoeing of horses. Joseph Cyrus opened a carpenter shop. John Robertson had a woodenware shop. Robertson, along with his Black assistant, Caesar, turned out spinning wheels and carved bowls.[10]

Colonel Richard Taylor brought his family to Louisville and built a house. He also brought his nine-month-old son, Zachary. In 1783, Colonel John Campbell built a tobacco warehouse below the Falls at Shippingport. Also in 1783, Evan Williams started a distillery at Fifth and Water Streets in Louisville, the first commercial distillery in Kentucky. Williams claimed the right to sell his whiskey without a license, but in 1788, he was indicted for his offense. Williams, a Louisville Board of Trustees member in Louisville, always brought a bottle of his whiskey for use at the meetings. It was always drained dry by the board members, so he did not worry about heavy fines for selling his liquor without a license.[11]

Mark Thomas was the first businessman to erect a tavern at the Falls of the Ohio. He owned Square Number 7 between Sixth and Seventh Streets and the river and Main Street, where he built a double log cabin two stories tall. John Nelson, Patrick Joyes, Edward Tyler, John Harrison,

Andrew Heth, William Pope and James Fontaine were also tavern keepers in early Louisville.[12]

In 1783, George Leech opened the first school in Louisville on Twelfth Street on Lot 90. Leech, an Englishman, was educated to become an Episcopal minister. He taught the classics and English studies. Leech later became a judge in the Northwest Territory. During that same year, Jacob Myers built an early church on Main and Twelfth Streets where all denominations could worship.[13]

Although Louisville was becoming a profitable city, not everything was calm. In June 1780, British colonel Henry Bird took six hundred Canadians and Native Americans, along with a cannon, and invaded Kentucky and destroyed Martins' and Ruddles' Stations, murdering or taking the residents as captives. In July 1780, General George Rogers Clark, with an avenging army of one thousand Kentuckians, comprised mostly of Louisville and Beargrass Stations citizens, invaded the Native American towns of Chillicothe and Piqua in Ohio and destroyed their homes and crops in retaliation for the raid on Martins' and Ruddles' Stations. In March 1781, a band of Native Americans killed Colonel William Linn, Captain Abraham Tipton, Captain John Chapman and several others. Captain Aquila Whitaker raised a company and went in pursuit. On August 15, 1782, English officers led six hundred Native Americans to attack Bryant's Station. They were not able to take the fort and retreated toward Blue Licks, or so the pursuing Kentuckians thought. The Kentuckians were overtaken at the Upper Blue Licks, where a battle erupted and the Kentuckians were completely defeated. In November, General Clark led an army of one thousand men, mostly Louisville residents, and crossed the Ohio River. The Native Americans were defeated. On April 12, 1783, Colonel John Floyd was shot by a Native American while riding from Spring Station to his own station on Beargrass Creek. He later died of his wounds.[14] In 1786, a small band of Native Americans entered Jefferson County and made its way to Hughes Station on Floyd's Fork, which is now called Long Run. They approached the land of Abraham Lincoln, the grandfather of the future sixteenth president. Lincoln had bought four hundred acres of land on March 4, 1780. In May 1786, Lincoln was planting a crop of corn with his sons, Josiah, Mordecai and Thomas, when they were attacked by the Native Americans. Between Hughes Station and his land, Lincoln was shot and killed by one of the Native Americans.[15] Josiah ran to the station for help, and Mordecai and Thomas ran to the cabin. Mordecai emerged from the cabin with a rifle and managed to kill one of the Native Americans as

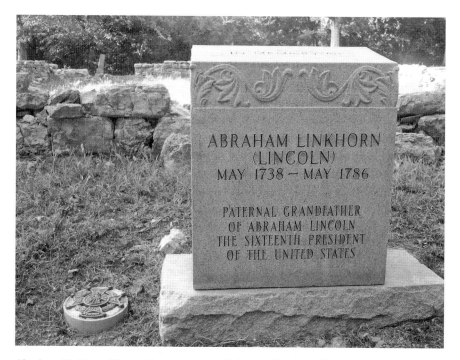

Abraham Linkhorn (Lincoln), paternal grandfather of Abraham Lincoln, sixteenth president of the United States, buried at Long Run Cemetery, Jefferson County. *Courtesy of the author.*

he was preparing to scalp his father. Men from Hughes Station pursued the retreating Indians.

Despite the area's unsettled status as a result of British-led raids and Native American attacks, business was booming in the city. Louisville's chief specialties were rope made at the several leading ropewalks and the making of well-constructed flatboats, which left Louisville's ports loaded with furs. The furs reached New Orleans and then were shipped to European markets.

In April 1792, the Commonwealth of Kentucky became the fifteenth state admitted to the United States. At the time, Louisville had two hundred houses. With statehood, new settlers flowed into Kentucky through the Cumberland Gap on the Wilderness Road. Others traveled into Louisville on the Ohio River. Tobacco was legal tender and exchanged throughout Kentucky and Virginia. In 1797, the city of Louisville elected its trustees. Archibald Armstrong, Gabriel Johnston, John Eastin, Evan Williams, Rueben Eastin, Henry Duncan and Richard Prather were elected the first trustees. Evan Williams became the first harbormaster. In 1801, Thomas Prather and James McConnell raised enough money to build the first bridge over Beargrass Creek; the following year, Asahel Linn and James Hunter completed the bridge. On January 18, 1801, the *Farmers Library*, a weekly newspaper edited by Samuel Veil, was printed for the first time. It lasted until 1808, when Veil decided to give up the newspaper industry and join the army. In 1814, he was promoted to captain and fought in the Battle of New Orleans and was brevetted major for his gallant conduct.

On October 14, 1803, Meriwether Lewis and William Clark met in Louisville and formed one of the most famous and successful partnerships in history. On October 26, Lewis and Clark, together with the nucleus of the Corps of Discovery, embarked down the Ohio River from Clarksville, Indiana. On their journey was a Black slave named York. He was the only African American on the expedition and the first African American to cross North America to the Pacific. York was William Clark's lifelong body servant.[16]

In 1804, Fortunatus Crosby and George Wilson were authorized to plan for a market house, which was built in the center of Market between Fourth and Fifth Streets. Market became the location for market houses. In 1806, the *Western American*, the second newspaper in Louisville, was started by F. Peniston. Only a few issues were published when Peniston decided to move to St. Louis. On November 6, 1806, Meriwether Lewis and William Clark stopped at Locust Grove and were entertained by Clark's brother-in-law and sister, William and Lucy Croghan.[17] In 1808, the *Louisville Gazette* was published by James Gray and David Rannals. In 1810, Nicholas Clark published the *Western Courier* and E.C. Barry published the *Louisville Correspondent*. The same year, the Jefferson County census listed 4,347 slaves, 1 free Black man, 13,399 Whites and 113 Indians. Louisville was ranked the second-largest city in the state, with a population of 1,357. The largest commercial project was the Hope Distillery Company, with a capital cost of $100,000. It was the first distillery to substitute machinery for hand power.[18]

In 1807, John James Audubon, the naturalist, ornithologist and painter, came down the river from Pittsburgh, Pennsylvania, and set up a general store with Jean Ferdinand Rozier. In 1808, he married Lucy Bakewell. He advertised separately from the general store that he would instruct any citizens of Louisville who might be interested in the art of drawing and would also paint portraits of citizens.[19] In 1810, while in Louisville, he met Alexander Wilson, the author of a great work on American

The *York* statue was sculpted by Ed Hamilton, with plaques commemorating the Lewis and Clark Expedition and York's participation in it. The statue is located at the Riverfront Plaza, next to the wharf on the Ohio River.

York Statue, designed by Ed Hamilton and erected in 2003, located at the Louisville Belvedere. *Courtesy of the author.*

ornithology. They became friends, but the friendship was short-lived when Audubon grew in recognition for his work on ornithology through his paintings, while Wilson's work in the field of ornithology was barely recognized in Louisville. On March 23, 1810, Wilson wrote that he was leaving Louisville because "he neither received one act of civility from those to whom I was recommended, one subscriber, nor one new bird, though I received my letters, ransacked the woods repeatedly, and visited all the characters likely to subscribe."[20] Audubon declined to subscribe to his publication, *American Ornithology*.[21] Audubon spent more than a decade as a businessman in Louisville.[22]

Portland Museum
2308 Portland Avenue
https://portlandky.org/exhibitions/from-collections /
502-776-7678

The Portland Museum covers nearly two hundred years of Kentucky culture, from the chartering of Portland as an independent town along the Falls of the Ohio to today's contemporary Portland neighborhood as well as moments in early cultural history that pre-date European settlers. The museum is located at Beech Grove, which is an 1852 Italianate residence on an estate along the historic Louisville & Portland Turnpike. With a modern addition built onto the front of the residence, the preservation of the original house displays a piece of Kentucky's architectural history as a unique, touchable exhibit within the museum. There are also two rotating exhibition galleries and a John James Audubon Gallery on the residence's first floor. The modern addition houses the museum's permanent exhibit; an architecture gallery; three rotating mini-galleries focused on Portland's art, heritage and community; a third rotating exhibition gallery; a workshop space for arts and public history education; a media room featuring a newsreel of the tragic 1937 flood; and the museum's gift shop. In addition, the museum's printmaking studio, located on the first floor of Beech Grove's former servants' building, is equipped with various Chandler & Price presses, cases of foundry type, screen printing equipment and bookbinding equipment. Most of the printmaking studio's equipment and accessories are part of the museum's collection, but the museum also utilizes the studio to engage children and adults in various printing and book arts techniques. One of the permanent exhibitions is Portland: The Land, the River, and the People, which allows visitors to discover how the nineteenth-century town of Portland, Kentucky, came into existence below the Falls of the Ohio River and the town's relationship with Greater Louisville. The exhibition employs dioramas, a terrain model, historic figures and automated lights and sounds to bring fascinating characters and events to life. The museum also has an animated Captain Mary Miller. The "lady steamboatman" greets museum visitors with tales of her life as the first woman in the United States licensed to captain a steamboat. The mannequin is a classic animatronic skillfully modeled after images of Captain Miller, who

This page: Portland Museum, 2308 Portland Avenue. *Courtesy of Steve Wiser.*

was honored in 2017 by the City of Louisville through the naming of the *Mary M. Miller*, a 350-person riverboat deemed the little sister of the *Belle of Louisville*.[23]

In 1811, Robert Fulton built the *Orleans* steamboat in Pittsburgh, and in October, the *Orleans* undertook its maiden voyage down the Ohio. On board were Nicholas Roosevelt, his young wife, an engineer, a pilot, six hands and a few domestics, and their dog Tige. Four days later, the steamboat arrived in Louisville, having taken seventy hours to make the seven-hundred-mile voyage. Also in 1811, the first Catholic church in Louisville was built on the northwest corner of Main and Tenth Streets.

In 1812, the streets in Louisville received their names, such as Water, Jefferson, Green, Walnut and South, which was later named Chestnut. That same year, the Methodists built their first church on the north side of Market, between Seventh and Eighth Streets. In 1813, Paul Skidmore started an iron foundry. Also in 1813, money was raised to pave the streets. In 1815, the work of paving Main Street from Third to Sixth was finished at a cost of six dollars per square. Also in 1815, John and Louis Tarascon began the foundation for the first flour mill in Louisville and Jacob Lewis started the Lewis Pottery not far from the river's edge on Bill Goat Strut Alley.

Louisville Stoneware & Company

731 Brent Street
https://www.stonewareandco.com/heritage / 502-582-1900

Louisville Stoneware & Company has a long history. In 1815, Jacob Lewis started Lewis Pottery and made thirty-gallon crocks, which held grain and was sealed with beeswax. He also produced butter churns, bowels and plates. By the 1840s until Prohibition, Louisville had become the bourbon capital of the world. Louisville's stoneware industry produced jugs to contain bourbon for general stores. Bourbon was delivered in wooden barrels, and customers brought the stoneware jugs to be filled. The jugs became advertising promotions with the name of the saloon or tavern stamped on them. During the Civil War, stoneware pottery and their storage containers were used by the Union army. As stoneware fell out of favor for tin and glass containers, Lewis Pottery changed hands several times. In 1905, S.O. Snyder bought John Bauer's pottery plant on Preston Street between Woodbine and Hill, which made pickle crocks and butter churns. Snyder changed the name to Louisville Pottery. In

Louisville Stoneware and Company, located at 731 Brent Street. *Courtesy of Steve Wiser.*

1908, Snyder moved the plant to 228 East Bloom Street. In 1936, John B. Taylor bought the Lottery Pottery and formed the J.B. Taylor Company. He became a major supplier of dishware, flowerpots and bakeware. In 1970, when Taylor died, John Robertson bought the company and changed the name to Louisville Stoneware and moved the company to 731 Brent Street. In 1997, Christy Lee Brown took over the company; Stephen A. Smith took over in 2007. Visitors can take a tour of the factory, paint their own pottery and buy some of the most popular patterns, such as the Bachelor Button.[24]

In 1816, the Presbyterians built their first church on the west side of Fourth, between Market and Jefferson Streets. In 1836, the church burned to the ground. Also in 1816, the *Governor Isaac Shelby*, the first steamboat built in Louisville, was launched. Captain L.L. Shreve, a Louisville resident, launched the steamboat *Washington*, which did trade between Louisville and New Orleans. Also in 1816, the Kentucky legislature incorporated the "Louisville Library Company" with Mann Butler, William C. Galt, Brooke

Hill, Hezekiah Hawley and William Tompkins as managers. The library was located in the second story of the south wing of the courthouse. In 1838, the books were given to the Kentucky Historical Society. In 1842, the five hundred books went to the Mercantile Association. They were given to the Louisville Library in 1847. They then traveled to the Kentucky Mechanics Institute (1854), the Young Men's Christian Association (1867), the Public Library of Kentucky (1870) and, finally, the Library of the Polytechnic Society (1878).[25]

In 1817, Samuel Drake built a theater on the north side of Jefferson between Third and Fourth Streets. The theater was three stories high and could hold eight hundred patrons. In 1818, Shadrach Penn issued the first edition of the *Public Advertiser*, which became the most famous newspaper in the area. On June 23, 1819, President James Monroe and General Andrew Jackson visited the city. The Louisville Light Horse militia, commanded by Captain Todd, and the Louisville Light Infantry, commanded by Captain Sturgus, escorted the dignitaries to their apartments. A huge banquet was held in their honor at the Washington Hall. Several days later, they had another dinner at Union Hall.[26]

By 1820, Louisville was a thriving and prosperous little town, with 670 buildings, and of these were 65 licensed stores and the remainder were small shops and homes.

General George Rogers Clark had been relieved of command by the governor of Virginia because the state was broke. He returned to his parents' home in Louisville and tried to collect money that he used to equip his troops. After his parent's death and the turn of the century, Clark moved across the Ohio River and founded the town of Clarksville on a land grant given to him by the state of Virginia. Ill health, due to exposure in the Northwest campaign, was followed by partial paralysis, which resulted in a badly burned leg when he fell near his fireplace, resulting in an amputation in 1809. After the amputation, Clark's sister, Lucy Clark Croghan, the wife of Major William Croghan, took him to live with her in a house near Louisville called Locust Grove. He died there on February 13, 1818. He was buried in the Croghan family plot at Locust Grove but was later reinterred in Cave Hill Cemetery.[27]

Locust Grove Historic Home
561 Blankenbaker Lane
http://locustgrove.org / 502-897-9845

Locust Grove was built in 1790 by William Croghan and his wife, Lucy Clark Croghan. William and Lucy, along with Lucy's brother General George Rogers Clark, welcomed America's leading dignitaries, including Presidents James Monroe and Andrew Jackson, John James Audubon, Cassius Marcellus Clay and Lewis and Clark. The home is currently a National Historic Landmark. The mission of Historic Locust Grove is to preserve and interpret the remaining fifty-five acres of William Croghan's estate, with its circa 1792 house, outbuildings, collection and grounds as examples of early nineteenth-century frontier America, and to share the stories of the many people who contributed to the history of the site, emphasizing the experiences of George Rogers Clark, Revolutionary War hero and founder of Louisville. On July 24,

Locust Grove, 561 Blankenbaker Lane. *Courtesy of Steve Wiser.*

1961, the Commonwealth of Kentucky partnered with Jefferson County to buy the house and the remaining fifty-five acres and restore the house. The house is currently open to the public and open for tours.[28]

In 1819, Peterson & Company made soap and candles. It was the largest soap and candlemaker in the western United States, producing twelve thousand pounds of soap weekly and one thousand pounds of candles daily. John H. Clark and Company owned a steam manufacturing mill, which produced eighty barrels of flour a day. The factory was located on Jefferson Street. The Tarascon brothers spent $150,000 building a flour mill at Shippingport. The mill's power was supplied by the water from the Ohio River. In June 1819, several distinguished visitors paid Louisville a visit, including President James Monroe and Andrew Jackson. Alexander Pope entertained Jackson, who, while in Louisville, decided to run for president. The year before, the Chickasaw Indians ceded the Louisiana Purchase to General Jackson, and Kentucky gained 72,962 acres and added eight counties: Ballard, Carlisle, Fulton, McCracken, Graves, Hickman, Marshall and Calloway. Also in 1819, George Keats, the brother of the famous poet John Keats, and his sixteen-year-old bride, Georgiana, moved to Louisville. When his brother Tom died in 1820, he returned to England to settle Tom's estate and claim his inheritance. George invested his inheritance in a Louisville lumber mill. The mill turned out to the very successful, and he used his profits to invest in real estate and a flour mill. In 1835, he became very wealthy and built a mansion on the south side of Walnut Street (Muhammed Ali Street) between Third and Fourth Streets known as the Englishman's Palace. Keats became a very successful businessman and prominent citizen of the city. He died in 1841 and was buried in Western Cemetery but later was reinterred in Cave Hill Cemetery.[29]

In 1821, Louisville was divided into three wards; one fire engine with a suction hose was provided for each ward. In 1822, the city experienced its worst epidemic to date. The fever wiped out entire families. Doctors called attention to the ponds in the city with rotting vegetable matter and the resulting pestilence. After the disease had taken its toll in the summer months, the residents of Louisville set about to make sure that the fever would never occur again. The city drained the ponds and removed the filth and cleaned the city completely. Louisville was never an unhealthy city again.

The city had been called the "Graveyard of the West" in the past, but after the citywide cleanup, it became one of the healthiest places in the country.[30]

On May 11, 1825, Louisville entertained French general Marquis de Lafayette. On his way to Louisville, his steamboat *Mechanic* caught a snag and sunk. Luckily, the steamboat *Paragon*, which was on the way from Louisville to New Orleans, changed course and picked up Lafayette and the rest of his passengers. Unfortunately, Lafayette lost his luggage. He was given the best dinner the city could afford at Washington Hall, and all the American Revolutionary heroes shook his hand. In 1824, the Episcopalians completed Christ Church on Second Street. In 1894, the church became the Cathedral of the Episcopal Diocese of Kentucky and currently is the oldest church in Louisville.[31] On January 12, 1825, the Louisville and Portland Canal Company was incorporated by the legislature, and work began in March 1826. In 1830, at a cost of $750,000, the canal was completed and opened to navigation.

The Louisville and Portland Canal (McAlpine Locks and Dam)
805 North Twenty-Seventh Street
https://www.lrl.usace.army.mil/Missions/Civil-Works/
Navigation/Locks-and-Dams/McAlpine-Locks-and-Dam /
502-574-2992

The two-mile Louisville and Portland Canal (now known as McAlpine Locks and Dam) was completed in 1830 and bypassed the Falls of the Ohio. The federal government purchased the Portland Canal in the nineteenth century, and in May 1874, Congress passed a bill allowing the Corps of Engineers to take full control of the canal. A new lock was built in 1921, and in 1962, the Portland Canal was renamed the McAlpine Locks and Dam after undergoing extensive modernization. The canal was the first major improvement to be completed on a major river of the United States. In October 2003, McAlpine was designated a Historic Civil Engineer Landmark by the American Society of Civil Engineers. The McAlpine Locks underwent a ten-year, $278 million expansion that was completed in 2009. Today, visitors can read interpretive panels and watch the locks in operation.[32]

Opposite: The Louisville and Portland Canal (McAlpine Locks and Dam).

Right: Original marker for the Louisville Portland Canal, showing James Guthie as president. The marker is in a section of the original Portland Canal wall, which was preserved by the United Corps of Engineers at the McAlpine Locks and Dam. *Courtesy of the author.*

In 1826, the *Focus* newspaper was started by W.W. Worseley and merged with the *Louisville Journal*. On February 13, 1828, an Act of Incorporation was passed and Louisville was declared a city. Shippingport became part of the city. Portland would not be annexed yet. A mayor and a city council of men were elected. On May 4, 1828, John Bucklin became the first mayor of Louisville. W.A. Cooke was elected the first marshal. In 1829, Bucklin opened the first public school, located on the upper story of the old Baptist church on the southwest corner of Fifth and Green Streets, which had been completed around 1828. The first principal was Mann Butler; his assistant was Edward Baker. The following year, the first city schoolhouse was built on the corner of Fifth and Walnut, and in 1830, the school was moved to Fifth and Green Streets.[33]

Chapter 3

THE AGE OF STEAMBOATS COMES TO LOUISVILLE

1830-1840

S teamboats had advanced rapidly from 1811 to 1830. In 1811, the *New Orleans* arrived in Louisville. The *Comet* was the second boat to arrive in Louisville (1813), and after that came the *Vesuvius*. In 1815, the *Enterprise*, built by Henry Shreve, came upriver from New Orleans to Louisville. It was the first steamboat to arrive at the Falls of the Ohio from New Orleans. In 1816, a group of Louisville businessmen built *The Governor Isaac Shelby*, which was the first steamboat to be launched from the Beargrass harbor. Also in 1816, Shreve built a boat specifically for the western rivers called the *Washington*. In 1818, the Louisville and Cincinnati Packet Line, known commonly as the United States Mail Line, which ran between Cincinnati, Louisville and St. Louis, was founded. Ten years later, a daily service was established between Louisville and Cincinnati. In 1824, the *General Pike* was completed. It was the first steamer for the exclusive use of passengers. The ship operated primarily between Cincinnati, Ohio and Louisville. It was commanded by Jacob Strader, who became the first president of the U.S. Mail Line. When steamboats took the place of flatboats and barges, Louisville's economy boomed as it shipped tobacco, hemp, whiskey, nails and gunpowder to New Orleans and the returning steamboats brought coffee and other luxuries. The steamboat helped to create Louisville's mercantile economy. In 1830, the city's population reached 687,000 residents, making it the largest city in the state. In 1834, James Howard began building boats at Shippingport. After several years, he moved his prosperous business across the river to Jeffersonville and started his shipyards.[34]

Howard Steamboat Museum
1101 East Market Street, Jeffersonville, Indiana
http://www.howardsteamboatmuseum.org / 812-283-3728

In 1834, nineteen-year-old James Howard started a shipyard on the banks of the Ohio in Jeffersonville, Indiana, and began to build his first boat, the *Hyperion*. During its three-generation, 107-year history, the Howard Shipyard would put more than three thousand vessels in the running waters of the Ohio and establish the largest inland shipyard in America. The story of the hardworking Howards and their famous riverboats is preserved and presented by the Howard Steamboat Museum, housed in the century-old Howard Mansion. The massive, twenty-two-room Romanesque Revival mansion was built adjacent to the old Howard Shipyard in 1894. The location of the mansion allowed easy access for James Howard's stable of craftsmen to help in the home's construction, and their fine hand is evident in the interior gingerbread woodwork

Howard Steamboat Museum, 1101 East Market Street, Jeffersonville, Indiana. *Courtesy of the author.*

and the grand staircase, reminiscent of those built in the elegant Howard steamboats. Visitors can admire the mansion's late-Victorian interior and see original artifacts from famous steamboats, such as the *Alice Dean,* the *Robert E. Lee* and others.

The most notable native of Shippingport was the Kentucky giant Jim Porter, who was seven feet, nine inches tall and weighed three hundred pounds. He was born on December 15, 1811, in Portsmouth, Ohio, and moved to Shippingport with his family when he was an infant. His father worked at the Tarascon Mill. At the age of fourteen, Jim was a jockey at the Elm Tree Garden horse track in Shippingport, but when he turned seventeen, folklore has it that he grew an inch in one day. By age thirty, he had reached his full height and weight. He was a cooper and later a hackney driver on the Portland and Louisville Turnpike and, in 1836, opened his first tavern, the Lone Star Coffee House, in Shippingport. In 1848, he built the Big Gun Tavern, the grandest hotel in the South.[35]

In 1830, George Prentice came to Louisville from New England and established the *Louisville Daily Journal.* In 1836, the Louisville Legion was formed and became a distinguished military rifle unit composed of the finest young men in the city. The regiment fought in the Mexican War. In 1858, the Louisville Legion reorganized and fought for the Union under the command of General Lovell Rousseau. In 1837, the financial panic affected Louisville and the state of Kentucky. Banks refused to honor specie payments. The Kentucky legislature suspended banks and refused to compel them to resume specie payments or to forfeit their charters.

On January 27, 1830, the Kentucky legislature chartered the Lexington and Ohio Railroad, which was the first railroad in the state and the first west of the Allegheny Mountains. October 22, 1831, the first rail was laid with a grand ceremony on Water Street in Lexington. Three years later, on January 25, 1835, the railroad linked with Frankfort. It finally completed its link with Portland in 1838, but the initial streetcar service was a failure, because the rail was unpopular with hackmen. Traffic dwindled. By 1839, the Lexington and Ohio Railroad service had ceased operating on a regular basis.[36]

During the 1830s, two new hotels were built in the city. The Louisville Hotel (1832) was the city's first large hotel. In 1835, the Galt House opened. It was considered the finest hotel in the United States. Major Aris Throckmorton ran the Galt House. The old Galt House was located at Second and Main Streets. The food served at the hotel was of superior quality and offered

Kentucky Historical Society Interpretive marker, Louisville Legion front side of marker. *Courtesy of the author.*

Kentucky Historical Society Interpretive marker, Louisville Legion, back side of marker. *Courtesy of the author.*

a great variety. It served mutton with currant jelly, redhead duck, stuffed woodchuck with hunter's sauce, wild goose with Potwine sauce, Bridge of Buffalo Tongue à la Godar, Arcade of Pheasants with green peas, boar's head, fish, soups, nine hot baked meats, nine roast meats, thirty-six entrees, six kinds of game, breads, relishes, fifteen vegetables, thirty kinds of confections, jellies, nuts, cakes and puddings.[37]

The Galt House
140 North Fourth Street
https://www.galthouse.com/gallery/our-hotel/
502-589-5200

In 1835, Aris Throckmorton built the first Galt House. The 60-room hotel stood on the northeast corner of Second and Main Streets. In the nineteenth century, the Galt House was acclaimed as Louisville's best hotel. Many noted people stayed at the original Galt House, including Jefferson Davis, Charles Dickens, Abraham Lincoln and Ulysses S. Grant. During the Civil War, the Galt House was utilized for meetings of Union generals. In September 1862, the hotel was the scene of an unusual murder, when General Jefferson D. Davis (not to be confused with Confederate president Jefferson F. Davis) shot Union general William "Bull" Nelson after a dispute. The first Galt House burned down in 1865. In 1869, a larger Galt House was built on the corner of First and Main Streets. The hotel closed in 1919 and was demolished in 1921. A new building was erected on the old site, which became the headquarters for the Belknap Hardware and Manufacturing Company. In 1972, the current Galt House was built. The hotel is a twenty-five-story, 1,300-room hotel and is the only hotel on the Ohio River. Views of the river are available to guests. It features the Terrace Room, a fitness center, a restaurant and the Conservatory. The largest hotel in Kentucky, the Galt House is also the official hotel of the Kentucky Derby, Churchill Downs, the Kentucky Oaks, the Kentucky Derby Festival, Thunder over Louisville and the KFC Yum! Center.[38]

This page: Galt House, 140
North Fourth Street, Louisville,
Kentucky. *Courtesy of the author.*

In 1840, the Louisville Gas Company lit up the city. That same year, the Belknap Hardware and Manufacturing Company started. Also in 1840, Louisville experienced its first great fire. The fire originated on the west side of Third Street, between Main and Market, in John Hawkins's chair factory, and burned south to the rear of the city post office and spread to the northwest corner of Third and Market. The fire spread north toward Main and burned every building west from the corner of Third to within two doors of the stone Bank of Louisville, which now houses Actors Theater. The fire crossed the street and spread to Third Street. Thirty buildings were lost in the fire. In 1842, the Jefferson County Courthouse opened. In 1846, the Law Department of the University of Louisville opened. Nine years later, the Louisville Medical Institute opened. The Medical Institute later became the University of Louisville. In 1846, Sarzedas & Bates built a theater on the southeast corner of Fourth and Green Streets. It enjoyed a great reputation for twenty years. In 1848, Cave Hill Cemetery opened and became the second-largest cemetery in the county.[39]

Cave Hill Cemetery

701 Baxter Avenue
https://www.cavehillcemetery.com/about/cemetery/early_ history / 502-451-5630

Cave Hill Cemetery was chartered in 1848 on William Johnston's Cave Hill Farm. It was a rural or garden-style cemetery. During the Civil War, 0.65 acres of ground was sold to the federal government for the burial of Union soldiers. Local Confederate sympathizers bought land nearby for Confederate soldier burials. In 1888, the cemetery purchased an additional 300 acres. The cemetery is a national arboretum, contains a national cemetery and is in the National Register of Historic Places. Cave Hill is also Louisville's premier cemetery. The Cave Hill Heritage Foundation's purpose is to secure funding for the long-term preservation of this unique cemetery. Specifically, the mission of the foundation is threefold: "To restore the historical monuments and buildings." Cave Hill Cemetery is known for its exquisite collection of monumental art, many examples of which are more than 150 years old. Additionally, the property includes a variety of historic structures, from the administrative office to the board room to the three-and-a-half-mile wall of brick and stone that encircles the perimeter. The resources provided through the foundation will allow cemetery management to be proactive both in addressing specific, long-term conservation projects and in responding to critical situations that require immediate intervention and stabilization. "To preserve the arboretum setting." On average, fifty trees are removed each year at Cave Hill Cemetery due to disease, old age or weather damage, and more than one hundred plants are replaced. The Cave Hill Heritage Foundation will help provide resources for the unexpected, as well as help preserve and sustain the beauty of the cemetery's arboretum setting. It will provide for the removal and the replacement of specimen trees and shrubs to ensure that future generations will have access to this amazing green space in the heart of Louisville. "To provide community education and awareness." The history of Cave Hill Cemetery is inextricably tied

Satterwhite monument. *Courtesy of the author.*

Colonel Harland Sanders monument, located at Cave Hill Cemetery. *Courtesy of the author.*

to the history of Louisville. Through its landscape and monuments, the cemetery tells the story of this beloved city by the river and its remarkable citizenry. The Cave Hill Heritage Foundation will help provide resources to produce educational materials, expand public awareness and develop special events and programs for schoolchildren and the community at large. It will also ensure that the critical task of recording and archiving the history of the cemetery will continue. Cave Hill Cemetery is open to the public and offers a wide variety of programs, including guided tours and different events throughout the year, such as the Cocktails on the Lawn event.

United States Marine Hospital
2215 Portland Avenue
http://marinehospital.org

In 1852, the United States Marine Hospital, located in the Portland neighborhood, began accepting patients. The history of the Marine Hospital dates to 1837, when the U.S. Congress authorized the construction of seven hospitals that would treat seamen and boatmen who became ill or were injured. A stipulation for the building of these hospitals was that they had to have a view of water. The hospital was constructed between 1845 and 1852. During the Civil War, the hospital remained largely closed, though it did take care of Union soldiers from battles at Shiloh and Perryville, which occurred early in the war. In late 1869, Mother Mary Ignatius Walker and five other Sisters of Mercy took over operations of the hospital until 1875, when it was reorganized and resumed as a Marine Hospital. By the turn of the twentieth century and into the 1920s, the majority of patients at the hospital were veterans of the First World War. The hospital remained serving the

United States Marine Hospital, 2215 Portland Avenue. *Courtesy of the author.*

boatmen of the area but expanded to care for patients from the U.S. Coast Guard and other federal employees. The hospital operated until 1933, when President Herbert Hoover made appropriations to build a new hospital behind the first one. By the middle of the twentieth century, the city of Louisville had purchased the property and used it as office space until the 1970s. Since then, the hospital has remained unused. In 1997, however, the United States Marine Hospital was placed in the National Register of Historic Places. It is one of the last remaining antebellum Marine Hospitals.[40]

In the 1850s steamboats ruled the rivers. Steamboats became floating palaces and had the best taverns and restaurants. The vessels had gold-etched ceilings and skylights of stained glass. Pianos were in the lounges and the staterooms had the finest sheets. But the steamboat was slowly approaching its golden age and would soon be replaced with the railroad.

Chapter 4

LOUISVILLE BECOMES A PROSPEROUS CITY AND THE RISE OF RAILROADS

1850–1860

During the 1850s, Louisville became a vibrant and wealthy city, but underneath the success, the city harbored racial and ethnic problems. In 1850, Louisville became the tenth-largest city in the United States. Its population rose from 10,000 in 1830 to 43,000 in 1850. Louisville became an important tobacco market and pork-packing center. By 1850, the city's wholesale trade totaled $20 million in sales. The Louisville–New Orleans river route held top rank on the entire western river system in freight and passenger traffic.[41] Not only did Louisville profit from the river, but also, in August 1855, its citizens greeted the arrival of the locomotive *Hart County* on Ninth and Broadway. The first passengers arrived by train on the Louisville and Frankfort Railroad (L&F). James Guthrie, president of the L&F, pushed the railroad along the Shelbyville Turnpike (Frankfort Avenue) through Gilman's Point (St. Matthews) and on to Frankfort. The track entered Louisville on Jefferson Street and ended at Brook Street. Leven Shreve, a Louisville civic leader, became the first president of the Louisville and Nashville Railroad. With the railroad, Louisville could manufacture furniture and export the goods to southern cities. Louisville was well on its way to becoming an industrial city. The Louisville Rolling Mill built girders and rails, and Louisville made cotton machinery, which it sold to southern customers. Louisville built steamboats, and the city hosted an ironworking industry with a plant on Tenth and Main called Ainslie, Cochran, and Company.[42]

In the 1850s, Louisville became the commercial center of the state. The city became an important tobacco market, became the second-largest city in terms of packing pork and produced over $20 million of general wholesale products. Louisville also manufactured hemp rope and cotton bagging. Cotton bagging was made of hemp, and hemp was also used to bale cotton. Hemp was Kentucky's leading agricultural product from 1840 to 1860, and Louisville was the nation's leading hemp market. Louisville made jean cloth for the slave market. The business area of Louisville stretched from Water (now River Road) to East (or Brook) Streets and from Market to Seventh Streets. Louisville's main commerce broke down into wholesale groceries, dry-goods houses and drug wholesalers. The city had eight pork houses, slaughtering and packing three hundred thousand hogs a year. Tobacco outranked meatpacking as Louisville's chief product, and the three main warehouses was located at Boone, Pickett and Ninth Streets. Dennis Long and Company was the largest pipe manufacturing company in the West. The cement manufactured in the city was the best in the country. The Louisville Rolling Mill Company, under the presidency of Thomas Coleman Sr., was the largest in the city and made boilers, bar and sheet iron and bolts for railroad bridges, which allowed Louisville to be independent of other cities for its supplies for steamboat building and allowed the company to trade its products in the South and West. The Fulton Foundry of Glover, Galt, & Company manufactured steam engines and machine castings of all kinds. B.F. Avery & Company, Munn's and Brinly, Dodge and Company made many of the plows in the South and Southwest. Christopher and Stancliffe made doors, sashes and railroad cars. The Peter Bradas Company made cough drops from a formula given by Jenny Lind. Cornwall and Brother made soap and candles. It also introduced glycerin into commerce. Needham's Marble Shop carried Italian, Egyptian, Irish and Sienna marble. McDermott and McGrain made a cooking stove called the "Durable Kentuckian." Wallace, Lithgow, and Company's Eagle Foundry made stoves and grates. Bridgeford and Holbrook, later D&J Wright, manufactured stoves and grates. The Falls City Foundry also made stoves. John Bull made his Fluid of Sarsaparilla and sold the drink to New Mexico and Cuba. Hays, Craig, and Company made the city's finest furs and peltries. The largest printing firm in Louisville was John P. Morton and Company. The paper used in the printing and publishing company, located at Tenth and Rowan, came from Alfred Victor and Antoine Bidermann du Pont. Isaac Cromie had the largest paper mill in the West, located on Main between Tenth and Eleventh Streets. Charles

Duffield & Company claimed to have the largest establishment devoted to the curing of hams, not only in the United States but also in the world. Milne & Binder were lithographers, and Peters, Webb & Company was extensive publishers of music. They also made pianos and organs. Hays and Cooper were extensive manufacturers of wagons, plows and castings for agricultural purposes.[43]

The steamboat route from Louisville to New Orleans held the top position for western river freight and passenger traffic, and the Louisville–Cincinnati route was the most crowded and most prestigious. Between August 25, 1848, and August 31, 1849, sixty-six different steamboats made 213 trips from Louisville to New Orleans. Between July 1854 and October 1855, Louisville shipbuilders constructed forty-one steamers. The steamboat industry employed 350 men building twenty-two boats a year and repairing another fifty. The Louisville Rolling Mill not only made boilers and machinery for the construction of steamboats, it also made cotton machinery for the South. More important, the mill began to make iron rails, bridge girders and steam boilers for trains. A new industry began to take shape in the city. By the mid-1850s, Ainslie, Cochran, and Company, located on Tenth and Main, had built a plant in order to meet the ever-increasing demand for steam engines, cotton gin machinery, wheels and castings for railroad cars. The firm claimed that its plant was the largest in the West.[44]

Railroads began to overtake steamboats. In 1850, the city chartered the Louisville and Nashville Railroad. Louisville had connections with Cincinnati, Pittsburgh, St. Louis, Memphis, Vicksburg and New Orleans. A river ferry to Jeffersonville or New Albany connected with the rail lines extending to St. Louis and Missouri, to east of Pittsburgh and north to the Great Lakes. Louisville had lines extending to Memphis, Nashville and Knoxville. The line to Lexington eventually extended to Virginia. The Louisville railroad also linked with the Baltimore and Ohio Railroad. Another rail line that ran to Louisville was the Louisville, New Albany, and Chicago Railroad, which ran two trains daily to St. Louis, Chicago and Cincinnati. When Louisville connected with Nashville, Louisville became the "Gateway to the South." Leven Shreve, a Louisville civic leader, became the first president of the L&N Railroad, but James Guthrie took control in 1860 and opened the railroad to 269 miles. Guthrie worked on plans for draining the ponds and setting up a better sanitary system. As Kentucky's commonwealth attorney, he was able to push through many reforms, and as a member of the state legislature, he managed to grant access for several turnpike companies and pushed through the construction of roads and the canal. He was the director and later president of the Bank of Kentucky and was instrumental in making the Louisville Medical Institute a part of the University of Louisville. Guthrie promoted the building of the Louisville and Nashville Railroad. He also was a Democrat who served in the Kentucky House of Representatives. In 1831, he was elected to the Kentucky state senate. Guthrie also ran for U.S. Senate several times and won in 1865 but resigned due to ill health in 1868. He had been secretary of the treasury under President Pierce and served as president of the University of Louisville in 1847.[45]

Louisville had three packet companies connecting it with Cincinnati, Nashville and New Orleans. Five stage routes ran to Taylorsville, Bardstown, Shelbyville and to Frankfort, Shawneetown and Nashville.[46]

The city established a board of health, which enacted a College of Physicians and Surgeons. The city had four hospitals and an ambulance. St. Joseph's Infirmary was located on the east side of Fourth Street between Chestnut and Broadway. The Louisville Marine Hospital, or the City Hospital, was located on Chestnut between Preston and Floyd. Two hospitals were located in Portland. The first hospital, the United States Marine Hospital, on High Street, was constructed in the 1840s. The second was the Alms House, located on Twenty-Eighth and Duncan. The St. John's Eruptive Hospital was on the Seventh Street Turnpike.[47]

Between 1850 and 1860, the first telegraphic communication between Louisville and New Orleans was established and the first mule-drawn streetcars were put into service. In 1854, the city formed the Louisville Water Company, and in 1857, work began on a reservoir and pumping station. A total of twenty-six miles of pipes were lid in the area between Main, Ninth, Broadway and Preston.[48]

Louisville Water Company Pump Station
3005 River Road
https://www.louisvillewater.com/WaterTowerPark /
502-897-1481

On October 16, 1860, the Louisville Water Company became the first public water provider in Kentucky. Chief Engineer Charles Hermany, along with Steam Engineer E.D. Leavitt, designed the giant steam-powered pumping engine that was used in Louisville

This page: Louisville Water
Company Pump Station.
Courtesy of Steve Wiser.

and throughout the country. The first pumping station and water tower are still in existence and are National Landmarks. The Louisville Water Tower is one of the oldest standing towers in the nation. In 1890, the Great Cyclone tore off the tower at the base, resulting in the rebuilding of the tower. During the Great Flood of 1937, engineers put the steam engines back into service to pump water, allowing the city to have fresh drinking water during the flood. In World War I, the federal government chose Louisville as the site of Camp Zachary Taylor. One of the factors that led to this choice was the fresh drinking water, which prevented the soldiers from getting cholera. Today, the Louisville Water Tower serves as an educational facility, where students can learn the treatment process that takes water from the Ohio River and turns it into a glass of the best-tasting tap water in the nation.[49]

On October 15, 1860, the city turned on the two steam engines manufactured by Louisville's Roach and Long Foundry, which began to pump water into the pipes.

The volunteer fire department used hand pumps to put out fires, and many of the volunteer companies did cooperate in putting out fires in the city. In 1858, the Louisville Board of Fire Underwriters bought a steam-powered pumper from Cincinnati, and the city council disbanded the volunteer companies and replaced them with a corps of sixty-five professional firemen and twenty-three horses.

Louisville boasted of having several cultural centers, including the Louisville Theater and Masonic Temple at Green (now Liberty) and Mozart Hall on Fourth and Jefferson. There were also horse races, fairs, musical societies and literary clubs. The Louisville Theater, on Fourth and Green, allowed both Black and White patrons. The city held agricultural fairs and exhibitions, such as the Tobacco Fair and the Southwestern Agricultural and Mechanical Association Fair. For those who loved horse races, in 1858, the city offered the Woodlawn Race Course, also known as the "Saratoga of the West." The DuPont Artesian Well, located on Main and Twelfth Streets, offered hundreds of citizens the chance to partake of the healthy water. For sports, the city offered the YMCA, the Baseball Club, a Mechanics Library and gambling.[50]

On April 6, 1851, Jenny Lind, the "Swedish Nightingale," played at the Mozart Theater for two days. A coachload of appointed citizens met her ten miles outside of the city and hitched her four white horses to her carriage. Draped with flags, many of the buildings honored her arrival. Welcoming crowds cheered her arrival, and children with flowers greeted her as she departed her carriage for the house arranged for her stay in Louisville. She sang "The Last Rose of Summer" for the crowd.[51]

Louisville had two newspapers before the war, the *Louisville Courier* and the *Louisville Journal*, both located between Third and Fourth Streets. George Prentice founded the *Louisville Journal*. He was a member of the Whig Party and later the American Party. He loved the Union, although he loved slavery. The *Louisville Courier*, owned by Walter Halderman, supported the Kentucky Democrats. The official editor of the newspaper after 1859 was Colonel Robert McKee. A third newspaper, the *Louisville Democrat*, was owned and edited by John H. Harney. It supported the northern Democrats. The paper was one of the few that promoted anti-slavery.[52]

Fifteen hotels occupied Louisville. At Second and Main was the famous Galt House. Other hotels were the National Hotel (Fourth and Main), the Louisville Hotel (Main and Sixth) and the United States Hotel (Eighth and Main).[53]

Louisville had two hundred taverns or coffeehouses. One of the better restaurants was Pargney's at 412 Third Street. W.A. Clark served European meals at his home on Fourth between Main and Market. The Crystal Palace at Fifth and Jefferson supplied merchants, hotels and families. The two most exclusive eateries were C.C. Ruefer's at St. Charles Restaurant (203 Fifth Street) and Walkers, or Cauweins (231 Third Street). Located on Seventh and Jefferson was Hafer's Ice Cream Saloon.[54]

On July 9, 1850, President Zachary Taylor died in Washington, D.C., after being in office for only sixteen months. Known as "Old Rough Ready," he was the nation's twelfth president. He was born in Virginia but brought to Kentucky when he was nine years old. In 1812, he defended Fort Harrison and served in the Black Hawk War of 1832, and in 1837, the federal government made him commander in Florida, where he defeated the Indians at the Battle of Okeechobee. During the Mexican War, he won the Battles of Palo Alto, Resaca de le Palma and Buena Vista. He was buried in the family burial site, now Zachary Taylor National Cemetery.

Zachary Taylor National Cemetery
4701 Brownsboro Road
https://www.cem.va.gov/cems/nchp/zacharytaylor.asp /
502-893-3852

Located in Jefferson County, Kentucky, in northeast Louisville, this cemetery was established in 1828 by an act of Congress initiated by the Taylor family to have the government take title of the family burial site where President Zachary Taylor was interred. Two donations of land from the state of Kentucky increased the original half acre Taylor plot to the national cemetery's present size of sixteen acres. Although the Taylor plot, which includes a tomb and mausoleum, is encompassed within the walled cemetery, the family plot does not belong to the United States. Despite the best efforts of the Taylor family, the U.S. Army judge advocate general decided against federal possession. The Taylor family burial ground is cared for and maintained by the National Cemetery Administration.[55]

This page: Zachary Taylor National Cemetery, 4701 Brownboro Road. *Courtesy of Steve Wiser*.

In 1854, Louisville engineers moved the channel of Beargrass Creek from where the creek flowed into the Ohio between Third and Fourth Streets to its present position opposite Towhead Island.[56] Louisville was the first city in the West, and the fifth in the country, to be supplied with gas. By 1859, there were thirty-five miles of mains and 925 streetlights. The city also had seven hundred miles of streets, alleys and sidewalks.[57] In 1859, the Jefferson County Court House was opened to the public. James Guthrie started building the courthouse in 1839; it took him twenty years to complete the project. The building, of classic Greek Revival style with Doric portico, was constructed with limestone and designed by Gideon Shyrock. James Guthie hoped the courthouse would become the Kentucky state capitol, but that never materialized.

Jefferson County Court House
600 West Jefferson Street
https://louisvilleky.gov/government/mayor-greg-fischer/history-metro-hall-building / 502-574-2003

Construction on the courthouse began in 1837, and both the City of Louisville and Jefferson County governments starting using the courthouse in 1842. Slave trading was conducted near the courthouse in the 1840s, as were speeches calling for the abolition of slavery. During the American Civil War, the building was used as the state capitol when Frankfort was seized by Confederate forces for three weeks. After a fire in 1905, the building was renovated by Brinton Davis. In 1972, the building was listed in the National Register of Historic Places. Extensive renovations took place in the 1980s. In 1980, the Jefferson County Courthouse Annex at 517 Court Place was listed in the National Register. The Jefferson County Courthouse, or Louisville Courthouse, was renamed Louisville Metro Hall. It currently houses the offices of the mayor of Louisville Metro. Also housed in the building are the offices of the Jefferson County Clerk, the Kentucky Court of Appeals and the Kentucky Supreme Court Justice for the Louisville district. There are two prominently sited statues outside the courthouse. In front of the building is a statue of Thomas Jefferson by Moses Jacob Ezekiel, given to the city in 1901. The second, on the corner of Sixth and

Above: Jefferson County Courthouse, located at 600 West Jefferson Street. *Courtesy of the author.*

Left: The raising of the Union flag over the Jefferson County Courthouse on Washington's birthday, February 1861. *Courtesy of the author.*

Jefferson and across from Louisville City Hall, is a statue of King Louis XVI. It was destroyed in 2020. The statue had been presented as a gift to Louisville from Louisville's sister city, Montpellier, France, on July 17, 1967.[58]

In 1853, the Mechanics' Institute was organized and supported a course of lectures and accumulated a library of five thousand volumes. In March 1853, President Millard Fillmore visited Louisville on his way to New Orleans. He boarded the palatial steamboat *Robert J. Ward*, piloted by Silas F. Miller.

European emigrants flowed into the city from Germany and Ireland. By 1850, 359,980 immigrants had arrived in America; by 1854, 427,833 immigrants had arrived to seek out a new living. With the massive amounts of immigrants into the city, native Louisville residents began to harbor anti-foreign, anti-Catholic sentiments. In 1841, the rise in the number of Catholics entering the city prompted the archdiocese to move the bishop's seat from Bardstown to Louisville. The archdiocese began construction on a new Catholic cathedral in Louisville, the Cathedral of the Assumption. Work was completed in 1852.[59]

In 1843, a new party came on the political scene, the American Republican Party. On July 5, 1845, the party changed its name to the Native American Party and held its first national convention in Philadelphia. The party opposed liberal immigration. On June 17, 1854, the Order of the Star Spangled Banner held its second national convention in New York City. The membership comprised "native Americans" and anti-Catholics. When its members answered questions about the group, they responded with, "I know nothing about it," earning the party the name Know Nothing, or Native American Party. The new political party gained national support. The Know Nothing Party encouraged and tapped into the nation's prejudice and fear that Catholic immigrants would take control of the United States and hand the nation over to the pope. By 1854, the Know Nothing Party had gained control of Jefferson County's government. The ethnic tension came to a boil in 1855, during the mayoral election. On August 6, 1855, Louisville experienced "Bloody Monday," in which Protestant mobs bullied immigrants away from the polls and began rioting in Irish and German neighborhoods. Protestant mobs attacked and slaughtered at least twenty-two people. The rioting began at Shelby and Green (Liberty) Streets and progressed through the city's East End. The mob burned houses on Shelby and headed for William Ambruster's brewery in the triangle between Baxter Avenue and Liberty Street and set the place ablaze. Ten Germans were burned to death. Quinn's Irish Row on the north side of Main between Eleventh and Twelfth Streets was burned, and some of the tenants burned to death; others were killed by rifle fire. The Know Nothing Party won the election in Louisville and in many other Kentucky counties.[60]

Slavery also became a topic of discussion among Louisville citizens. With the Kansas-Nebraska Act of 1854, slavery became a hot issue among politicians. The 1792 Kentucky Constitution legalized slavery, and by 1800, the tax lists showed 40,000 slaves in the state. By 1808, the federal government had banned the slave trade, but the selling of women, children and men continued, and by 1830, Blacks made up 24 percent of Kentucky's population. The Non-Importation Act of 1833 halted the transfer of Black persons for resale, but Kentucky repealed the act in 1849, and slave markets expanded in the state. The Arterburn brothers kept slave pens near Second Street between Market and Main, and iron-barred coops held slaves ready to be shipped south. Chained slaves marched up Main Street to board boats in Portland to be shipped to New Orleans. Although slavery was on the way out in Louisville by 1850, the city sold an increasing number of Kentucky slaves south. Kentucky annually exported between 2,500 and 4,000 slaves. Amazingly, Louisville also had a free Black population and a handful of free African Americans who managed to acquire property. Washington Spradling, freed from slavery in 1814, became a barber and, by the 1850s, owned property valued at $30,000. In 1857, free Blacks and slaves held a New Year's Eve Ball and rented facilities from the Fall City Hotel. Louisville was a city that had aspects of the agricultural South and aspects of the North with the rise in industry and the railroads.[61]

In 1860, the population of Louisville was 68,030. During that year, the House of Refuge was opened. Louisville had 436 factories employing 7,396 people, paying out $2,120,000 a year in wages and turning out a product worth $14,135,000 a year. Machinery and ironworks manufactured $830,000 in capital a year, making the product number one; soap and candles accounted for $332,000 of production; tobacco and cigars turned out $121,600 in annual products; agricultural implements accounted for $143,000 worth of product; gas accounted for $422,950; iron rolling mills accounted for $250,000 worth of annual capital; and books made up $81,000 worth of capital. Interestingly, alcohol accounted for $70,000 in capital.

By 1860, Louisville's population had increased to 69,739, of which 4,903 were slaves. There were 26,120 foreign-born residents, half coming from Germany. The Louisville and Portland Canal underwent improvements to allow larger steamboats. The city wharf also underwent renovations.[62]

On January 1860, the city board passed a street railroad ordinance. The Louisville and Portland Company added new railcars onto its lines.

By 1860, Louisville had several Catholic churches, including St. Aloysius, Notre Dame du Port, St. Boniface, St. Patrick's, St. John's and the Cathedral of the Assumption. The Episcopals had Christ Church Cathedral, or St. Paul's. In 1860, Calvary Church was built. For Baptists, the Walnut Street Baptist Church at Fourth and Walnut had 478 members. The German Evangelical Lutherans established St. Paul's Church on Preston and Green. The Unitarians built a church on Fifth and Walnut, and the Jewish congregation established its church on Fourth just south of Green.[63]

As for schools, Louisville had fifteen schools with 134 teachers. Louisville had Male High School. The general assembly legalized its name as the

Academical Department of the University of Louisville. A four-year classical course was offered to students in obtaining a BA and an English course recommended to those who wanted to become architects, engineers or manufacturers. A BS degree was offered on completion of the course.[64]

The Female High School was located on Ninth and Chestnut. There were also several private schools, including the English and German Academy, B.B. Huntoon's School for Boys, Mrs. Lanham's Female Academy, the Locust Grove Academy, Mrs. Eliza Field's Female School, Reverend George Beckett's Institution for Young Ladies, the Louisville Mercantile Academy and the Louisville Commercial College.[65]

The University of Louisville (Eighth and Chestnut) comprised the School of Law and Medicine. The law school was one of six in the country that required two years of study for the degree. The Kentucky Medical School (Fifth and Green) was considered one of the most elegant colleges in the country.[66]

Louisville citizens also enjoyed Jacob's Woods, located south of Broadway between First and Fourth, and Preston Wood's at Broadway and Underhill. The Phoenix Hill Brewery was also a favorite hangout for Louisville citizens.[67]

Louisville had eight banks with a capital of $9,530,000. The three largest were the Bank of Louisville, the Bank of Kentucky and the Commercial Bank. Banker's Row was located on Main Street between Second and Fifth Streets. In 1858, the city completed the Custom House and Post Office at the southwest corner of Third and Liberty.[68]

In the November 1860 presidential election, the state gave native Kentuckian Abraham Lincoln less than 1 percent of the vote. Kentuckians did not like Lincoln, because he stood for the eradication of slavery and his Republican Party aligned itself with the North. But Kentuckians also did not vote for native son John C. Breckinridge and his Southern Democratic Party, which most of the country regarded as secessionists. In 1860, Kentuckians owned 225,000 slaves, with Louisville's slaves comprising 7.5 percent of the population, but Kentucky also loved the Union. Kentucky wanted to keep slavery and stay in the Union. Most Kentuckians, including residents of Louisville, voted for John Bell of Tennessee of the Constitutional Unionists Party, which stood for preserving the Union and keeping the status quo on slavery, or Stephen Douglas of Illinois, who ran on the Democratic Party ticket. Louisville cast 3,823 votes for John Bell. Douglas received 2,633 votes. On December 20, 1860, South Carolina seceded from the Union, other southern states followed, and by early 1861, eleven southern states had left the Union—except Kentucky. Senator Henry Clay worked for compromise, and the state followed his lead.

Chapter 5

LOUISVILLE DURING THE CIVIL WAR

1861-1865

On February 22, 1861, the pro-Union citizens of Louisville decided to celebrate George Washington's birthday. Union flag-raising spread throughout the city, and Louisville became known as the "City of Flags."[69] The event took on a whole new meaning with the political situation. The citizens of Louisville decided to raise the national flag with pomp and circumstance over the Jefferson County Court House. Fifty thousand people attended the event at the courthouse. At 2:30 p.m., the Louisville Battalions formed on Jefferson Street, fronting the courthouse.

Colonel J.H. Harvey and George D. Prentice, editor of the *Louisville Journal*, raised the national flag over the courthouse. Colonel William Woodruff and the Marion Rifles, a Louisville militia company, fired three volleys from their muskets. When the citizens of Louisville raised the flag, General Simon B. Buckner, commander of the Kentucky State Guard, gave no order to salute as required by the published program and patriotic duty. Buckner and a large portion of his command moved from the courthouse yard. Colonel William Woodruff saluted the national colors.[70] Divisions among the Kentucky State Guard and the local pro-Union militias began to divide over which side the state would chose—Union or Confederate.

On April 12, 1861, Confederate brigadier general Pierre G.T. Beauregard ordered his cannons to be fired on Fort Sumter, in the Charleston, South Carolina harbor, starting the Civil War. The commander of Fort Sumter was Union major general Robert Anderson of Louisville, Kentucky. After the firing, President Abraham Lincoln called for 75,000 volunteers, but Kentucky governor Beriah Magoffin refused to send any men to act against the Southern states, and Unionists and secessionists supported his position. On April 17, 1861, Louisville hoped to remain neutral and spent $50,000 for the defense of the city, naming Lovell Rousseau as brigadier general. Rousseau formed the local Louisville Home Guard. Unionists asked Lincoln for help, and he secretly sent arms to the Louisville Home Guard. The U.S. government sent a shipment of weapons to Louisville and kept the rifles hidden in the basement of the courthouse. As with the rest of the state, Louisville residents were divided as to which side they should support. Louisville Main Street wholesale merchants dealt with the South with steamboats traveling the Ohio River from Louisville to New Orleans and supported the Confederacy. Blue-collar workers, small retailers and professional men, such as lawyers, supported the Union. On April 20, two companies of Confederate volunteers left by steamboat to New Orleans. Five days later, three more companies departed for Nashville on the L&N Railroad. Union recruiters raised troops at Eighth and Main, and the Union recruits left for Indiana to join other Union regiments.[71]

On May 20, 1861, Kentucky declared its neutrality. The L&N's depot on Ninth and Broadway in Louisville and the steamboats at Louisville wharfs sent uniforms, lead, bacon, coffee and war material south. Lincoln did not want to stop the city from sending goods south for fear of upsetting Kentucky's delicate balance of neutrality. But on July 10, 1861, a federal judge in Louisville ruled that the U.S. government had the right to stop shipments of goods from going south over the L&N Railroad.[72]

On July 15, 1861, the War Department authorized U.S. Navy lieutenant William Nelson to establish a training camp and organize a brigade of infantry. Nelson commissioned William Landrum, a colonel of cavalry. Theophilus Garrard, Thomas Bramlette and Speed Fry were commissioned with the rank of colonel in the infantry. Landrum turned his commission over to Lieutenant Colonel Frank Wolford. Garrard, Bramlette and Fry established their camps at Camp Dick Robinson in Garrard County, and Wolford erected his camp near Harrodsburg, breaking Kentucky's neutrality.[73] Brigadier General Lovell Rousseau established a Union training camp opposite Louisville in Jeffersonville, Indiana, naming the camp after Joseph Holt. Governor Magoffin protested the establishment of the Union camps to Lincoln, but the president ignored Magoffin, stating that the will of the people wanted the camps to remain in Kentucky.[74]

In August 1861, Kentucky held elections for the State General Assembly and Unionists won majorities in both houses. But the residents of Louisville continued to be divided on the issue of which side to join. The *Louisville Courier*, under Walter Halderman, was very much pro-Confederate, while the *Louisville Journal*, under George Prentice, was pro-Union.

On September 4, 1861, Confederate general Leonidas Polk broke Kentucky's neutrality by invading Columbus, Kentucky. As a result of the Confederate invasion, Union general Ulysses S. Grant entered Paducah, Kentucky. Jefferson Davis allowed Confederate troops to stay in Kentucky. General Albert Sidney Johnston, commander of all Confederate forces in the West, sent General Simon Bolivar Buckner of Kentucky to invade Bowling Green. Union forces in Kentucky saw Buckner's move toward Bowling Green as the beginning of a massive attack on Louisville. With twenty thousand troops, General Johnston established a defensive line stretching from Columbus in western Kentucky to the Cumberland Gap, controlled by Confederate general Felix Zollicoffer. On September 7, the Kentucky legislature, angered by the Confederate invasion, ordered the Union flag to be raised over the state capitol in Frankfort, declaring its allegiance with the Union. The legislature also passed the "Non-Partisan Act," which stated that "any person or any person's family that joins or aids the so-called Confederate Army was no longer a citizen of the Commonwealth."[75] The legislature denied any member of the Confederacy the right to land, titles or money held in Kentucky or the right to legal redress for action taken against them.

With Confederate troops in Bowling Green, Union general Robert Anderson moved his headquarters to Louisville. On June 4, 1861, General George McClellan appointed Anderson as military commander for the district of Kentucky, and on September 9, the Kentucky legislature asked Anderson to be made commander of the Federal military force in Kentucky. The Union army accepted the Louisville Legion at Camp Joe Holt in Indiana into the regular army. Major John Delph sent two thousand men to build defenses around the city of Louisville. On October 8, Anderson stepped down as commander of the Department of the Cumberland. General William Tecumseh Sherman took charge of the Louisville Home Guard, and Lovell Rousseau sent the Louisville Legion along with another two thousand men across the river to protect the city. Sherman wrote to his superiors that he needed two hundred thousand men to take care of Johnston's Confederates. The Louisville Legion and the Home Guard marched out to meet Buckner's forces, but Buckner did not approach Louisville. His men destroyed the bridge over the Rolling Fork River in Lebanon Junction and, with the mission completed, returned to Bowling Green.[76]

Union troops arriving at the Louisville wharf, 1861. *Harpers Weekly. Courtesy of the author.*

Louisville became a staging ground for Union troops heading south. Troops flowed into Louisville from Ohio, Indiana, Pennsylvania and Wisconsin. White tents and training grounds sprang up at the Oakland track, Old Louisville and Portland. Camps were also established at Eighteenth and Broadway, along the Frankfort and Bardstown Turnpikes.

In January 1862, Union general George Thomas defeated Confederate general Felix Zollicoffer at the Battle of Mill Springs, Kentucky. In February, General Grant and Admiral Andrew Foote's gunboats captured Fort Henry and Fort Donelson on the Kentucky and Tennessee border. General Johnston's defensive line in Kentucky crumbled before his eyes. He had no other choice but to fall back to Nashville. No defensive preparations had been made at Nashville, so Johnson continued to fall back to Corinth, Mississippi.

Although the threat of invasion by Confederates subsided, Louisville remained a staging area for Union supplies and troops heading south. By May 1862, the steamboats arrived and departed at the wharf in Louisville with their cargoes. Military contractors in Louisville provided the Union army with two hundred head of cattle each day, and the pork packers provided thousands of hogs daily. Trains departed for the South along the L&N, but in July 1862, General Braxton Bragg, commander of the Army of Mississippi, and General Edmund Kirby Smith, commander of the Army of East Tennessee, planned an invasion of Kentucky. On August 13, 1862, Smith marched out of Knoxville with nine thousand men toward Kentucky and arrived in Barboursville, Kentucky. On August 20, 1862, Smith announced that he would take Lexington, Kentucky. On August 28, Bragg's army moved toward Kentucky. At the Battle of Richmond, Kentucky, on August 30, Smith's Confederate forces defeated Union general William "Bull" Nelson's Union troops, capturing the entire force, essentially

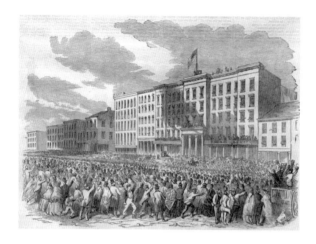

Top: The arrival of the Forty-Ninth Ohio Infantry, as it marches past the Louisville Hotel, October 19, 1861. *Harpers Weekly. Courtesy of the author.*

Bottom: Union general Don Carlos Buell's bodyguard parading east on Main Street at Fifth Street in January 1862. *Harpers Weekly. Courtesy of the author.*

leaving Kentucky with no Union support. Nelson managed to escape back to Louisville. Smith marched into Lexington and sent a Confederate cavalry force to take Frankfort, Kentucky's capitol.

General Don Carlos Buell's Union army withdrew from Alabama and headed back to Kentucky. General Henry Halleck, commander of all Union forces in the West, sent two divisions from General Grant's army, stationed in Mississippi, to Buell. Confederate general John Hunt Morgan of Lexington, Kentucky, managed to destroy the L&N Railroad tunnel at Gallatin, Tennessee, cutting off all supplies to Buell's Union army. On September 5, Buell reached Murfreesboro, Tennessee, and headed for Nashville. On September 14, Bragg reached Glasgow, Kentucky. On that same day, Buell reached Bowling Green. Bragg decided to take Louisville. One of the major objectives of the Confederate campaign in Kentucky was to seize the Louisville and Portland Canal, severing Union supply routes on the Ohio River. One Confederate officer suggested destroying the Louisville canal so completely that "future travelers would hardly know where it was." On September 16, Bragg's army reached Munfordville, Kentucky. Colonel James Chalmers attacked the Federal garrison at Munfordville, but he was in over his head, and Bragg had to bail him out. Bragg arrived at Munfordville with his entire force, and the Union force at Munfordville surrendered. Buell left Bowling Green and headed for Louisville.

Fearing that Buell would not arrive in Louisville to prevent Bragg's army from capturing the city, General William Nelson ordered the construction of a hasty defensive line around the city and the placement of pontoon bridges across the Ohio to facilitate the evacuation of the city or to receive reinforcements from Indiana. Two pontoon bridges, built of coal barges, one below the Big Four Bridge and the other from Portland to New Albany, were erected, but the Union army arrived to prevent the Confederate seizure of the city. On September 25, 1862, Buell's tired and hungry men arrived in Louisville. Bragg moved his army to Bardstown but did not take Louisville. He urged General Smith to join his forces to take Louisville, but Smith told him to take the city on his own.

With the Confederate army under Bragg prepared to take Louisville, the citizens of the city panicked. To make matters worse, General Nelson issued

Twelve thousand Union troops arriving from the advance army of the Army of the Ohio, September 24, 1862, along the Salt River Road (present-day Dixie Highway) as seen on Broadway, east of Eighteenth Street. *Harpers Weekly. Courtesy of the author's personal collection.*

the following order: "The women and children of this city will prepare to leave the city without delay." He ordered the Jeffersonville ferry to be used for military purposes only. Private vehicles were not allowed to go aboard the ferryboats without a special permit. Hundreds of Louisville residents gathered at the wharf to be transported to New Albany or Jeffersonville. With Frankfort in Confederate hands, the state legislature held its sessions in the Jefferson County Courthouse. Troops, volunteers and impressed labor worked around the clock to build a ring of breastworks and entrenchments around the city. New Union regiments flowed into the city. Nelson took charge of the defense of Louisville. He sent Union troops to build pontoon bridges at Jeffersonville and New Albany to speed up the arrival of reinforcements, supplies and, if needed, the evacuation of the city.[77]

Instead of taking Louisville, Bragg left Bardstown to install a Confederate governor at Frankfort. On September 26, 1862, five hundred Confederate cavalrymen rode into the area of Eighteenth and Oak and captured fifty Union soldiers. The following night, a heavy skirmish occurred just beyond Middletown on the Shelbyville Pike, and on September 30, Confederate and Union pickets fought at Gilman's Point in St. Matthews. The Union troops pushed the Confederates back through Middletown to Floyd's Fork.

The War Department ordered General Nelson to command the newly formed Army of the Ohio. When Louisville prepared for the Confederate army under Bragg, General Jefferson C. Davis, who could not reach his command under General Don Carlos Buell, met with Nelson to offer his services. Nelson gave him the command of the city militia. Davis opened an office and went to work in assisting in the organization of the militia. On September 20, 1862, General Davis visited General Nelson in his room at the Galt House. Nelson asked Davis if his brigade was ready for service, and Davis asked Nelson if he could obtain arms for them. Nelson asked Davis how many men were in his brigade. Davis responded that he had about 2,500 men. Nelson angrily barked to Davis: "About twenty-five hundred! About twenty-five hundred! By God! You a regular officer and come here to me and report about the number of men in your command? God damn you, don't you know, Sir, you should furnish me the exact number?" Davis told Nelson that he did not expect to get the guns now and only wanted to learn if he could get them and where and after learning the exact number of troops he would draw the needed weapons. Nelson flew into a rage and screamed at Davis: "About twenty-five hundred! By God I suspend you from your command, and order you to report to General Wright; and I've a damned mind to put you under arrest. Leave my room, Sir!" Davis told

Evacuation of Louisville. *Harpers Weekly. Courtesy of the author.*

General Nelson that he would not leave the room until he gave him an order. Nelson barked: "The hell you won't! By God I'll put you under arrest, and send you out of the city under a provost guard! Leave my room, Sir!" General Davis left the room and, in order to avoid arrest, crossed the river to Jeffersonville, where he remained until the next day, when General Stephen Gano Burbridge joined him. Burbridge had also been relieved of command by General Nelson under a trivial cause. General Davis came to Cincinnati with Burbridge and reported to General Wright, who ordered Davis to return to Louisville and report to General Buell and Burbridge to remain in Cincinnati. General Davis returned to Louisville and reported to Buell. When Davis saw General Nelson in the main hall of the Galt House fronting the office, he asked the governor of Indiana, Oliver Morton, to witness the conversation between him and Nelson. The governor agreed, and the two walked up to Nelson. General Davis confronted General Nelson and told him that he, Nelson, took advantage of his authority. Nelson, sneeringly and placing a hand to his ear, said: "Speak louder, I don't hear very well." Davis, in a louder tone, repeated his statement. Nelson indignantly told Davis that he did not take advantage of his authority. Davis told Governor Morton that Nelson threatened to have him arrested and sent out of the state under

Top: Union general William Bull Nelson. *Bottom*: Union general Jefferson Davis. *Courtesy of the Library of Congress.*

provost guard. Nelson took his own hand and struck Davis twice in the face and stated, "There, damn you, take that!" Davis left the room, but before he left, he told Nelson: "This is not the last of it; you will hear from me again." General Nelson turned to Governor Morton and asked if he had come to insult him, too. Morton stated that he had not come to insult Nelson but was requested that he be present and listen to the conversation between Nelson and Davis. Nelson violently told the bystanders: "Did you hear the damned rascal insult me?' and walked into the ladies' parlor. In three minutes, Davis returned with a pistol he had borrowed from Captain Gibson of Louisville and walked toward the door that Nelson had passed through. He saw Nelson walk out of the parlor and into the hall separating the main hall from the parlor, and the two faced each other ten yards apart. General Davis drew his pistol and fired, the ball entering Nelson's heart. General Nelson threw up both hands and grabbed a gentleman standing nearby around the neck and exclaimed, "I am shot!" Nelson walked up the flight of stairs toward General Buell's room but sank at the top of the stairs. Fellow officers took Nelson to his room and laid him on his bed. Nelson requested Reverend John Talbot to see him at once. Talbott administered the ordinance of baptism. The general whispered, "It's all over" and died fifteen minutes later.[78]

With General Nelson dead, the command switched over to General Buell. On October 1, 1862, the Union army marched out of Louisville with 60,000 men. Buell sent a small force to Frankfort to deceive Bragg as to the exact direction and location of the Federal army. The ruse worked. On October 4, the small Federal force attacked Frankfort and Bragg left the city and headed back for Bardstown, thinking the entire Federal force was headed for Frankfort. Bragg decided that all Confederate forces should concentrate at Harrodsburg, Kentucky, ten miles northwest of Danville. On October 8,

A highly overdramatized scene of the murder of Union general William "Bull" Nelson by Union general Jefferson C. Davis at the Galt House, October 1, 1862. *Harpers Weekly. Courtesy of author.*

Buell and Bragg fought at Perryville, Kentucky. Bragg's 16,000 men attacked Buell's 60,000. Federal forces suffered 845 dead, 2,851 wounded and 515 missing, while the Confederate toll was 3,396 dead. Although Bragg won the Battle of Perryville tactically, he wisely decided to pull out of Perryville and link up with Smith. Once Smith and Bragg joined forces, Bragg decided to leave Kentucky and head for Tennessee.

After the battle, the massive number of wounded flooded into Louisville. Hospitals were set up in public schools, homes, factories and churches. The Fifth Ward School, built at Fifth and York Streets in 1855, became Military Hospital Number Eight. The United States Marine Hospital also became a facility for wounded Union soldiers from the battle of Perryville. Constructed between 1845 and 1852, the three-story Greek Revival Louisville Marine Hospital contained one hundred beds and became the prototype for seven U.S. Marine Hospital Service buildings, including at Paducah, Kentucky, which later became Fort Anderson. Union surgeons erected the Brown General Hospital, located near the Belnap campus of the University of Louisville, and other hospitals were erected at Jeffersonville and New Albany, Indiana. By early 1863, the War Department and the U.S. Sanitary Commission had erected nineteen hospitals. By early June 1863, 930 deaths had been recorded in the Louisville hospitals and Cave Hill Cemetery set aside plots for the Union dead.

Louisville also had to contend with Confederate prisoners. Located at the corner of Green and Fifth Streets, the Union Army Prison, also called the Louisville Military Prison, took over the old "Medical College building." Union authorities moved the prison near the corner of Tenth and Broadway. By August 27, 1862, Confederate prisoners of war were flowing into the new military prison. The old facility continued to house new companies of provost guards. From October 1 to December 14, 1862, the new Louisville

Military Prison housed 3,504 prisoners. In December 1863, over 2,000 prisoners, including political prisoners, Federal deserters and Confederate prisoners of war, were located in the military prison. The facility was made of wood and covered an entire city block, stretching from east and west between Tenth and Eleventh Streets and bounded north and south by Magazine and Broadway. The main entrance to the prison was located on Broadway near Tenth. A high fence surrounded the prison, which had at least two barracks. The hospital was attached to the prison and consisted of two barracks on the south and west sides of the square with forty beds in each building. The Union commander at the Louisville Military Prison was Colonel Henry Dent, but in April 1863, military authorities replaced him with Captain Stephen E. Jones. In October 1863, military authorities replaced Captain Jones with C.B. Pratt.[79]

Just a block away from the Louisville Military Prison, Union authorities took over a large house on Broadway between Twelfth and Thirteenth Streets and converted it into a female military prison.

On September 22, 1862, Lincoln issued the Emancipation Proclamation, which declared that, on January 1, 1863, all slaves in the rebellion states would be free. Some Kentucky Union soldiers, including officers such as Colonel Frank Wolford of the First Kentucky Cavalry, quit the army over the declaration. The proclamation and the recruitment of slaves into the Union army ended the relationship between Lincoln and Kentucky. The controversy drove the state into the hands of the Democrats, who retained power for a century.

The Taylor Barracks, at Third and Oak in Louisville, recruited Black soldiers. Black Union soldiers who died from wounds or disease were buried in the Louisville Eastern Cemetery.

After the fall of New Orleans and the capture of Vicksburg, Mississippi, on July 4, 1863, the Mississippi and Ohio Rivers were open to Union boats without harassment. On December 24, 1863, a steamboat from New Orleans reached Louisville.

On June 10, 1863, General Braxton Bragg finally gave permission for Confederate general John Hunt Morgan's raid on Kentucky. Morgan met with Basil Duke and informed him that he was going to ignore Bragg's orders and continue his raid into Ohio. The next day, on June 11, Morgan took his division across the Cumberland to attack the garrison at Carthage.

Unfortunately, Bragg ordered Morgan to support General Buckner, who was threatened by a Union raiding party. Morgan spent three weeks moving east through Gainesboro and Livingston, then north across the Kentucky line to Albany. Morgan never encountered the raiding party. By July 2, the rains had stopped and Morgan's raid was back on track. On July 4, Morgan arrived at the Green River Bridge and found it heavily fortified by Colonel Orlando Moore and his Twenty-Fifth Michigan Infantry. Morgan's men heard the Michigan troops cutting down trees. Morgan demanded that Moore surrender; Moore replied that the Fourth of July was a bad day to surrender. Moore's force comprised four hundred men behind narrow breastworks one hundred yards long. Morgan ordered Captain Byrne's battery to fire on Moore's men. Morgan sent D.W. Chenault's Eleventh Kentucky Cavalry straight at the breastworks. Colonel Chenault was killed during the charge, and the men fell back. D. Howard Smith led his cavalry in a second wave, but the attack failed to dislodge the Union soldiers. Morgan called off the attack and turned for Lebanon. Morgan lost seventy-one men.

On July 4, General John Pemberton surrendered to General Grant at Vicksburg. On that same day, Robert E. Lee, with his Army of Northern Virginia, failed in his attempt to crush the Union army under General George Meade at Gettysburg.

On July 5, Morgan came upon Colonel Charles Hanson's Twentieth Kentucky Union regiment, supported by two Michigan regiments at Lebanon. Colonel Hanson refused to surrender. His men held the railroad depot. Morgan formed a two-line front and marched the men to the edge of the town. Hanson threw up a crude breastwork, and Morgan ordered his battery under the command of Captain Edward Byrne to fire on the Union breastwork. Colonel Roy S. Cluke's Eighth Kentucky assaulted the depot. Hanson was told to hold out, since reinforcements had arrived. Hanson's men pinned down the Eighth Kentucky. Cluke's men could not advance nor retreat. Lebanon was completely surrounded, and Morgan could not take the town, nor could he withdraw, until Cluke was safely brought back to Morgan's lines. Major Webber brought the Second Kentucky into the fight. The Second Kentucky fought up to the rear of the depot. Colonel Hanson surrendered. During the charge to take the depot, John Hunt Morgan's brother Lieutenant Tom Morgan was killed. The Union reinforcements arrived too late to save Colonel Hanson, but Morgan did not want to engage another Union force and rode off before the reinforcements could reach him.

Morgan's men rode on to Bardstown, Kentucky. While there, Morgan learned from his telegraph operator, George Ellsworth, that Union cavalry were gathering in his rear and were twenty-four hours away. The Yankees were certain that Morgan headed for Louisville, and troops were concentrating in the city. Morgan prepared the way for his crossing into Indiana at Brandenburg, Kentucky. He sent Captains Sam Taylor and Clay Merriwether and the Tenth Kentucky toward Brandenburg. They would find Captain Thomas Henry Hines somewhere around the town. They were to join Hines and take Brandenburg, including any boats docked at the harbor.

Morgan ordered Captain William Davis to take Company D, Second Kentucky, and Company H, Eighth Kentucky, on a diversionary expedition east of Louisville. Davis's mission was to cut telegraph wires, burn railroad bridges and create the impression that his two companies were actually Morgan's entire force. Davis's force was to take Twelve Mile Island above Louisville, cross the Ohio and attempt to rejoin Morgan's men at Salem, Indiana.

On July 7, Sam Taylor and Clay Merriwether led their companies into Brandenburg. The *John B. McCombs* steamed into the Brandenburg landing. Once the *McCombs* was tied to the wharf, forty Confederates jumped onboard the steamer and captured the ship. A few minutes later, the mail boat *Alice Dean* came steaming upriver. From the pilothouse of the *McCombs*, Merriwether ordered Captain Ballard of the *McCombs* to steam out toward the *Alice Dean*. The *McCombs* touched its bow with the *Alice Dean*, and the Confederates stormed aboard the *Alice Dean*, capturing the steamer.

Morgan and the Second Kentucky arrived in Brandenburg at 9:00 a.m., and Captains Taylor and Merriwether rode out to greet Morgan, informing him that they had captured two steamers and that Captain Hines had brought in the rest of his command. Morgan set up his headquarters at a house on the highest hill in town overlooking the river. He next ordered his men to begin crossing into Indiana. Captain Ballard of the *McCombs* and Captain Pepper of the *Alice Dean* were given instructions, and one of Morgan's Parrott rifles was placed on the ships.

Captain Hines and the Second Kentucky would board the steamers and cross the river first on the *McComb*, and Colonel W.W. Ward and the Ninth Tennessee would cross on the *Alice Dean*. The horses would be transported after the men arrived on the Indiana shoreline.

As the fog on the river lifted, a line of Indiana militia formed along the banks of the Ohio and opened fire with their muskets and a single six-pound cannon. Colonel Basil Duke found the Indiana militia's cannon through his field glasses and ordered Captain Byrne to fire with his remaining Parrott rifles and howitzers on the antiquated gun. The Indiana militia broke and ran from the accurate fire of Byrne's guns.

After the *McCombs* and *Alice Dean* unloaded the Second Kentucky and Ninth Tennessee, the *Alice Dean* began to re-cross the Ohio to the Brandenburg landing when the gunboat *Elk*, equipped with three howitzers, fired at the town, turned and then fired at the Confederate cavalry. Morgan ordered Captain Byrne to focus his Parrotts on the *Elk*. After about an hour's duel, the *Elk* turned around and headed back to Louisville. As soon as the *Elk* steamed out of sight, Morgan crossed the horses to the Indiana side of the river. By midnight, the rear guard had finished crossing into Ohio. Morgan ordered both steamers to burn, but the captain of the *McCombs* knew Basil Duke and escaped the torch. Captain Ballard promised to steam upriver to Louisville. As soon as Morgan's men began their raid in Indiana, Union cavalry arrived in Brandenburg but were helpless to stop Morgan.

On July 8, there was alarm in Louisville due to the approach of General John Hunt Morgan's Confederate cavalry. The city council ordered "the enrollment of all males between 18 and 45 into companies for services, if required, and all refusing to be enrolled would be sent to the North. Nearly five thousand men are enrolled and actively drilling."

On July 8, the Union military allowed the enrollment of Black troops.

Henry Magruder, a member of Morgan's command during the raid and part of the diversionary force, wrote that on July 11, Captain William Davis's two Confederate regiments destroyed as much of the Louisville and Lexington Railroad as possible and successfully diverted attention away from Morgan's main force. Captain Davis's men struck for the river at Westport, twenty-five miles above Louisville. When they arrived, they found the ferry guarded on the Indiana side, since most of the people thought that Morgan's main forces planned to cross at Westport. According to Magruder, Davis sent spies over the river in the guise of escaped prisoners, who told the Indiana guards that all of Morgan's men were on the other side of the river. The Indiana men rallied "by the hundreds, and there were men enough there to kill us with clubs."[80] Magruder and the rest of the spies left quietly and ran down to Twelve Mile Island, where they heard of a couple of barges moored to the island. Twelve of the men swam to the island and brought one of the boats over to the shore. The twelve men were sent over the river as an advance guard. The next trip in the boat brought the rest of Company D, and the boat reached the island with a part of Company H, when down the river the men saw "a turtle like thing, dark and threatening, come creeping on us. Presently a flash, a curl of smoke, then a deep report and a shell burst on the island."[81] The fire from the Federal gunboat *Moose* spooked the horses, and they broke for the Kentucky shore. Davis told his men that he would try to link up with Morgan with the men who were on the island side. Davis's men were in enemy territory, cut off from all support. Captain Davis captured the home guard pickets and made for the railroad. The men burned a bridge and arrived at a store and robbed the owner of $2,000. After they left the store, two Union cavalry regiments attacked Davis's men. The men ran for their lives, but their horses gave out. The Yankee cavalry overtook them, and Davis's men scattered in every direction. Magruder and seven other men managed to escape. The eight men consulted their next step, but home guards interrupted their meeting and attacked them. Magruder and the remaining men shook off their pursuers by hiding in the swamp. The men decided to break into two squads. Magurder, Morris, Hopkins and Cushingberry separated from the rest of the group. Magruder and his squad arrived at Mauckport, Indiana. The men seized a skiff and floated to the Kentucky side of the river. After a long trek, the four men safely made their way back to Tennessee.[82] General Manson's large force, transported on ten steamboats, managed to capture most of Captain Davis's men.

On July 26, General Morgan and his remaining forces surrendered at New Lisbon, Ohio, ending the longest raid of the Civil War; it accomplished very little. On July 31, Union general Ambrose Burnside declared martial law in Kentucky for the purpose of protecting only the rights of loyal citizens and the freedom of elections. No disloyal person would be allowed to vote.

On August 3, Thomas Bramlette was elected governor of Kentucky; Richard Jacob became his lieutenant governor. Only 85,000 of 140,000 Kentuckians cast their votes. Kentuckians refused to vote or were kept from the polls by military intimidation or interference and by threats or fears of arrest. In some counties, the military struck Democratic candidates from the poll books or the military arrested members on the Democratic ticket, because the military deemed them disloyal.

On September 24, twenty-one ladies met at a house. As a group of Rebel prisoners marched by the house, the ladies waved their handkerchiefs and shouted, "Hurrah for Jeff Davis!" The military authorities arrested the women and required them to take the oath of loyalty. Two women refused, and they spent the night in the Louisville Military Prison. By morning, the two women were more than happy to take the oath.[83]

The Southern sympathizers' underground headquarters was the house of J.J. Johnson between Sixth and Market Streets. On October 3, the *Louisville Democrat* began to side with the Southern cause and announced the release of three new books: *The Life of Stonewall Jackson*, *Confederate Official Reports of Battles* and *Southern History of the War*.

On October 25, President Lincoln exempted Kentucky from the enlistment of Black soldiers.

Between November 1 and November 11, 1864, the military issued 2,976 rations to families of soldiers and 125 rations daily to Southern refugees. Beggars in the streets increased; by mid-November, Louisville had become the "asylum of the poor of all sections."[84] On December 2, the military authorities established a depot on Second Street where daily rations could be issued to the destitute families of soldiers.

By 1864, Louisville's history had entered a dark period. Guerrilla warfare plagued the state, so the Radicals in Congress took a heavy hand to Kentucky. In Kentucky, a guerrilla was defined as any member of the Confederate army who destroyed supplies, equipment or money. Any returning Confederate was considered a guerrilla. On January 12, 1864, Union general Stephen Gano Burbridge of Kentucky succeeded General Jeremiah Boyle as military commander of Kentucky. On July 5, President Lincoln suspended the writ of habeas corpus, which meant that a person could be imprisoned without trial, their house could be searched without warrant and the individual could be arrested without charge. Lincoln also declared martial law in Kentucky, which meant that elected officials were powerless to act on behalf of their constituents. Civilians accused of crimes would be tried not in a civilian court but, instead, in a military court, in which the citizen's rights may not be guaranteed under the Constitution. On this same day, General Burbridge became military governor of Kentucky with absolute authority.[85]

On July 16, 1864, Burbridge issued Order No. 59, which declared: "Whenever an unarmed Union citizen is murdered, four guerrillas will be selected from the prison and publicly shot to death at the most convenient place near the scene of the outrages."[86] On August 7, Burbridge issued Order No. 240, by which Kentucky became a military district under his direct command. Burbridge could seize property without trial from persons he deemed disloyal. They could be shot without trial or question.

During the months of July and August, Burbridge set out to build more fortifications in Kentucky. As Union general William T. Sherman marched through Georgia, Kentucky no longer faced the threat from a Confederate army, but Burbridge felt the need to build earthworks. He received permission from Union general John Schofield to build fortifications in Mount Sterling, Lexington, Frankfort and Louisville. The plans furnished for each location called for a small enclosed fieldwork of about two hundred yards along the interior crest, with the exception of Louisville, which would be five hundred yards. Other earthworks would follow in Louisville as opportunity and the means available would allow. All the works were to be built by soldiers, except at Frankfort, where the labor was performed by the state, and at Louisville, by the city. Lieutenant Colonel J.H. Simpson of the Federal Engineers furnished the plans and engineering force. Eleven forts protected the city in a ring about ten miles long from Beargrass Creek to Paddy's Run. They included, from east to west: Fort Elstner between Frankfort Avenue and Brownsboro Road, near Bellaire, Vernon and Emerald Avenues; Fort Engle at Spring Street and Arlington Avenue; Fort Saunders at Cave Hill Cemetery; Battery Camp Fort Hill between Goddard Avenue, Barrett and Baxter Streets, and St. Louis Cemetery; Fort Horton at Shelby and Merriweather Streets (site of a present-day incinerator plant); Fort McPherson on Preston Street, bounded by Barbee, Brandis, Hahn and Fort Streets; Fort Philpot at Seventh Street and Algonquin Parkway; Fort St. Clair Morton at Sixteenth and Hill Streets; Fort Karnasch on Wilson Avenue between Twenty-Sixth and Twenty-Eighth Streets; Fort Clark at Thirty-Sixth and Magnolia; Battery-Gallup at Gibson Lane and Forty-Third Street; and Fort Southworth on Paddy's Run at the Ohio River (now the site of a city sewage treatment plant with a marker located at 4522 Algonquin Parkway). Also in the area was Camp Gilbert and Camp C.F. Smith, although the exact locations for both sites are lost to history. The first work built was Fort McPherson, which commanded the approaches to the city via the Shepherdsville Pike, Third Street Road and the Louisville and Nashville Railroad. The fort served as a citadel if an attack came before the other forts were completed. The fort could house one thousand men. General Hugh Ewing, Union commander in Louisville, directed that municipal authorities furnish laborers for fortifications, ordered the arrest of all "loafers found about gambling and other disreputable establishments" in the city for construction work and assigned military convicts to the work. Each fort was a basic earth and timber structure surrounded by a ditch with a movable drawbridge at the entrance, and each was furnished with an underground magazine to house two hundred rounds of artillery shells. The eleven forts occupied the most commanding positions to provide interlocking cross fire between them. A supply of entrenching tools was collected and stored for emergency construction of additional batteries and infantry entrenchments between the fortifications. The guns in the Louisville forts were never fired, except for salutes.

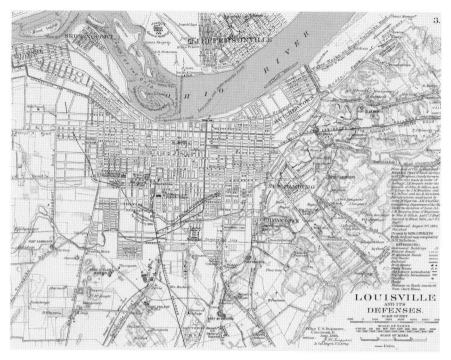

Original 1865 map of "Louisville and Its Defenses," by U.S. Corps of Engineers lieutenant colonel J.H. Simpson. *Original map courtesy of author.*

With Order Nos. 59 and 240, Burbridge began a reign of terror in Kentucky and Louisville. On August 11, he commanded Captain Hackett of the Twenty-Sixth Kentucky to select four men to be taken from prison in Louisville to Eminence, Henry County, Kentucky, to be shot for unknown outrages.

On October 25, 1864, Burbridge ordered four men—Wilson Lilly, Sherwood Hartley, Captain Lindsey Dale Buckner and M. Bincoe—to be shot by Captain Rowland Hackett of Company B, Twenty-Sixth Kentucky, for the alleged killing of a postal carrier by guerrillas allegedly led by Captain Jerome Clark (Sue Munday) near Brunerstown, present-day Jeffersontown, Jefferson County. On November 6, two men named Cheney and Morris were taken from the prison in Louisville and transported to Munfordsville and shot in retaliation for the killing of Madison Morris of Company A, Thirteenth Kentucky Infantry. James Hopkins, John Simple and Samuel Stingle were taken from Louisville to Bloomfield, Nelson County, and shot in retaliation for the alleged guerrilla shooting of two Black men. On November 15, two Confederate soldiers were taken from prison in Louisville to Lexington and hanged at the Lexington Fair Grounds in retaliation. On

November 19, eight men were taken from Louisville to Munfordsville to be shot in retaliation for the killing of two Union men.[87]

By the end of 1864, Burbridge had arrested twenty-one prominent Louisville citizens, plus the chief justice of the Kentucky State Court of Appeals, Joshua Bullitt, on treason charges. Many of the captured guerrillas were brought to Louisville and hanged on Broadway at Fifteenth or Eighteenth Streets.

By the November 1864 elections, Burbridge had tried to interfere with the election for president. Despite military interference, Kentucky citizens voted overwhelmingly for Union general George B. McClellan over Lincoln. Twelve counties were not even allowed to post their returns.[88]

As the Confederacy began to fall apart in January 1865, Burbridge continued his reign of terror. On January 20, Nathaniel Marks, formerly of Company A, Fourth Kentucky, C.S., was condemned as a guerrilla. He claimed that he was innocent but was shot by a firing squad in Louisville. On February 10, Burbridge's term as military governor came to an end. Secretary of War Edward Stanton replaced Burbridge with Major General John Palmer. On March 9, following a skirmish at Howard's Mill, Kentucky, Union authorities sent troops to Owingsville to chase several bands of guerrillas. On March 12, fifty Union soldiers from the Thirtieth Wisconsin Infantry under the command of Major Cyrus Wilson surrounded a tobacco barn ten miles south of Brandenburg near Breckinridge County. At daybreak, a Union soldier fired into the barn. Gunfire erupted from the barn, and four Union soldiers fell wounded. Inside the barn were the famous guerrilla Jerome Clarke (aka Sue Mundy), Henry Medkiff and Henry Magruder. Major Wilson had earlier injured Magruder at Howard's Mill. Wilson told Clarke that his men would be treated as prisoners of war if he surrendered. Clarke agreed, and Major Wilson escorted all three men to Brandenburg, where they boarded a steamer for Louisville. Military authorities kept Clarke's trial a secret, and the verdict had already been decided the day before the trial. On March 14, military authorities planned Sue Mundy's execution, even though the trial had not even started. At the brief hearing, Mundy "stood firm and spoke with perfect composure." He stated that he was a regular Confederate soldier and that the crimes he was being charged with had not been committed by him or had been committed by Quantrill. During the three-hour trial, Mundy was not allowed counsel or witnesses for his defense. Three days after his capture, Union authorities scheduled Clarke for public hanging just west of the corner of Eighteenth and Broadway in Louisville. On March 15, Reverend J.J. Talbott visited Clarke in prison and notified him that his "life's journey was nearing its end." The minister informed Clarke that he would be hanged that afternoon. Clarke knelt and prayed. He asked Talbott to baptize him in the cell. With Clarke dictating, the minister wrote four letters: one to Clarke's aunt, one to his cousin, one to a young lady named Lashbrook and, to his fiancée, he wrote: "I have to inform you of the sad fate which awaits your true friend. I am to suffer death this afternoon at 4 o'clock. I send you from my chains a message of true love, and as I stand on the brink of the grave I tell you I do truly, fondly love you. I am ever truly yours." Clarke made his last requests, stating that he wanted his body to be sent to his aunt and stepmother in Franklin next to his parents and that he be buried in his Confederate uniform. At 3:25 p.m., four handpicked companies of Union soldiers, dressed for parade, formed in front of the makeshift prison. Clarke, joined by Talbott and a guard, exited the prison and took their seats in a carriage for the ride to the gallows. Clarke wore a dark blue jacket with a row of Kentucky buttons, dark cashmere pants and boots.[89]

When the carriage arrived at the gallows, Clarke and Talbott exited and stopped at the foot of the gallows to pray. Clarke gave one last statement to the crowd. He said: "I am a regular Confederate soldier—not a guerrilla.…I have served in the Army for nearly four years.…I fought under General Buckner at Fort Donelson and I belonged to General Morgan's command when I entered Kentucky." In response to the charge that he as Sue Mundy killed helpless prisoners, he stated: "I have assisted in the capture of many prisoners and have always treated them kindly.…I hope in and die for the Confederate cause." After his neck was placed in the noose and the level was pulled, Clarke's neck did not break from the three-foot fall. He slowly strangled to death. According to witnesses, he struggled and convulsed so violently, Union authorities feared he would break the rope. Over fifteen thousand people attended Sue Mundy's execution. After authorities cut Mundy's body down from the scaffold, witnesses cut off his buttons as keepsakes. Police arrested three men for fighting over Mundy's hat. On October 29, 1865, Union authorities hung Henry Magruder behind the walls of the Louisville Military Prison, thus ending the careers of two famous Kentucky guerrillas.[90]

On April 9, 1865, General Robert E. Lee surrendered to General Ulysses Grant, and on April 14, General Joseph Johnston surrendered to General William T. Sherman, ending the Civil War.[91]

On May 15, 1865, Louisville became a mustering-out center for troops from midwestern and western states, and on June 4, military authorities established the headquarters of the Union Armies of the West in Louisville.

During June, 96,796 troops and 8,896 animals left Washington, D.C., for the Ohio Valley, where 70,000 men took steamboats to Louisville and the remainder embarked for St. Louis and Cincinnati. The troops boarded ninety-two steamboats at Parkersburg and descended the river in convoys of eight boats, to the sounds of cheering crowds and booming cannon salutes at every port city. For several weeks, Union soldiers crowded Louisville, and on July 4, 1865, General Sherman visited the city to conduct a final inspection of the Armies of the West. By mid-July, the Armies of the West had disbanded and the soldiers headed home.

After the war, Louisville returned to becoming an industrial city. Union general Jeremiah Boyle returned to the city to start the new Louisville City Railway. Plans were made to rebuild the Galt House on First and Main Streets. The Robert Rowell Electrotype Company was established, the first foundry south of the Ohio River. Josiah B. Garthright, a first lieutenant in General John Hunt Morgan's cavalry, built the saddle firm Gathright and Company.

On December 18, 1865, the Kentucky legislature repealed the Expatriation Act of 1861, allowing all who served in the Confederacy to have their full Kentucky citizenship returned without fear of retribution. The legislature also repealed the law that any person who was a member of the Confederacy was guilty of treason. Additionally, the Kentucky legislature allowed former Confederates to run for office. On February 28, 1866, Kentucky officially declared the war over. Louisville became the headquarters for the Military Division of the South, and soldiers remained in the city until the late 1870s. The constant presence of soldiers in the city after the war only increased the city's hatred toward military authorities.

What effect did the war have on the city? Fathers and sons were divided in their loyalties, brothers fought against brothers and neighbors against neighbors. In all, 67 generals from Kentucky fought for the Union and 38 for the Confederacy. During the conflict, 76,000 men from Kentucky served in the Union, and 25,000 men fought for the Confederacy. At every western theater battle, Kentuckians fought Kentuckians. In the war, 10,000 Kentuckians were killed in battle; 20,000 died from disease and exposure. Half of the Kentuckians who reached manhood in the 1850s and 1860s were either killed or disabled by the war. According to Kentucky historian Thomas Clark, after the war, "hatreds and enmities ran deep." The war ruined men, both spiritually and physically, "and crippled at least two future generations emotionally." With so much hatred toward the Union military, Louisville residents embraced Confederate officers, who entered law, insurance, real estate and political office.

As Robert McDowell stated in his book *City of Conflict*: "Louisville was sick of the butchery, sick of the greed of profiteers, sick of rowdy, drunken soldiers, sick of being treated like an occupied city by the Union of which she was supposed to be a part. She had no experience with Confederate armies. The only real combat soldiers knew were Union soldiers, and these had been inflicted on her for four years."

Louisville embraced the "Lost Cause" and saw the Confederate soldiers as fighting a just cause. Louisville searched for regional identity and found the South to be the perfect fit for its needs. George Yater, Louisville historian, agrees with McDowell: "The impact of the ex-Confederates was out of all proportion to their numbers. Louisville's gradual loss of enthusiasm for the war continued to be a potent factor in the city during the post war years. In addition, the bitterest memories were kept alive by the continued military presence."

Louisville erected a Confederate monument in 1895 near the campus of the University of Louisville, and the city hosted two Confederate veteran reunions, one in 1900 and another in 1905. There are no Union memorials in the city. On November 28, 2016, the Confederate monument was moved to Brandenburg, Kentucky.

Farmington Plantation
3033 Bardstown Road

Farmington is a fourteen-room Federal-style home that was the center of a nineteenth-century hemp plantation belonging to John and Lucy Speed. Designed from a plan by Thomas Jefferson and completed in 1816 using slave labor, the home is currently owned by Jefferson County and open for tours. On April 15, 1837, future president Abraham Lincoln met Joshua Speed, formerly of Farmington plantation in Louisville, Kentucky, who owned a general store in Springfield, Illinois. Their friendship lasted from April 1837 until Lincoln's death in April 1865. Joshua Speed became Lincoln's most devoted and closest friend, and his friendship with Lincoln carried over to his brother, James Speed.

Joshua and James Speed were the sons of John and Lucy Fry Speed of Jefferson County, Kentucky. The couple had eleven children. James Speed was born on March 11, 1812, and Joshua

Above: Farmington Plantation, 3033 Bardstown Road. *Courtesy of the author.*

Left: James Speed, attorney general from 1864 to 1866, lived at Farmington. *Courtesy of the Library of Congress.*

was born on November 14, 1814. Lucy devoted her life to educating her children. James became Lincoln's attorney general in 1864. Lincoln visited Farmington in 1841 for three weeks. During the Civil War, Joshua and James became Lincoln's unofficial informants on the state of affairs in Kentucky.

Chapter 6

LOUISVILLE DURING THE GILDED AGE

1870–1900

After the war, ex-slaves and immigrants supplied the labor force for the emerging factories in Louisville. Ex-Confederate soldiers took advantage of the opportunities in the thriving commerce center that was undamaged by the war and was not under a military government, and they found a community that embraced them and their "Lost Cause." Most of these men went into real estate, insurance and law. Louisville was the headquarters for the Military Division of the South until the federal government withdrew the troops from the southern states in the 1870s. Ex-Confederate soldiers such as Bennett Young, J.J.B. Hilliard, Basil Duke and John B. Castleman stayed in Louisville and became notable figures in Louisville's Gilded Age.[92]

Brennan House
631 South Fifth Street

The Brennan House is the only historic home remaining on a street once lined with similarly grand homes—an oasis of Victorian refinement amid Louisville's downtown business district. The three-story brick, Italianate townhouse features six bedrooms, expansive side verandas, a period garden and elegant interior finishes dating to the Victorian era. Constructed in 1868 by tobacco wholesaler Francis Slaughter Jones Ronald, the house was purchased in 1884 by Thomas Brennan for $12,000. It remained home to the Brennan

Brennan House, 631 South Fifth Street. *Courtesy of the author.*

family for seventy-five years. Thomas Brennan, a native of Ireland, made his fortune as an equipment manufacturer and inventor. He and his wife, Anna Bruce, had nine children, eight of whom survived into adulthood and grew up in the house. Two of the sons became doctors. In 1912, one of them, Dr. J.A.O. Brennan added a waiting room, office and examining room as a north wing to the house. The home is now a museum and furnished with an original family collection of the most luxurious and opulent furniture and decorative arts of the day and features a preserved early twentieth-century medical office.[93]

Louisville had the advantage of the Ohio River with its connection to many other navigable waterways. On February 18, 1870, the first bridge across the Ohio River at Fourteenth Street was completed; on March 1, the first train crossed the bridge. In 1886, the Kentucky and Indiana Bridge was the first multimodal span to cross the Ohio River and allowed both a railway and two wagon ways, which allowed wagons, streetcars, pedestrians and other animal-powered vehicles to cross into New Albany, Indiana, from Louisville. In 1895, the Big Four Bridge was completed. The six-span railroad truss bridge crossed the Ohio River, connecting Louisville with Jeffersonville, Indiana. The name came from the Cleveland, Cincinnati, Chicago, and St. Louis Railway.[94]

Thomas Edison House
729 East Washington

Built in 1850, the shotgun duplex located in the Butchertown neighborhood became the home of Thomas Edison when he lived and worked in Louisville. In 1866, at the age of nineteen, Edison traveled to Louisville to work as a telegraph key operator. With his skill at receiving telegraph messages, Edison acquired a job with the Western Union office, located at Second and Main Streets, about eight blocks from his home. In August 1866, he took up residence at East Washington Street. He was fascinated with the telegraph and how to improve its efficiency. In October 1867, Edison left

Thomas Edison House, 729 East Washington Street. *Courtesy of the author.*

Kentucky Historical Society marker located in front of the Thomas Edison House. *Courtesy of the author.*

Louisville. In 1879, he invented the incandescent light bulb. Edison and his company returned to Louisville in 1883 to install the light bulbs at the Southern Exposition Building. Today, the Thomas Edison House serves as a museum, housing artifacts that Edison invented, including light bulbs, cylinder and disc phonographs and an Edison Kinetoscope, which was the first home motion-picture projector. The museum also has a chronology of his life, including some of his most significant inventions. Also included in the timeline are major national and international events.[95]

With the advent of railroads, Louisville had cheap and easy communication with the important points on the continent, including connections with cities in the North, South, West and along the seaboard. The Louisville & Nashville Railroad was chartered on March 2, 1850, and the first train ran 185.23 miles to Nashville in November 1859. In 1870, the Knoxville branch was opened to Lexington. On February 24, 1860, the Bardstown branch of the Louisville and Nashville Railroad was completed. In November 1868, the Richmond line was completed. On January 19, 1877, the Cecilian branch was completed, the Glasgow Branch under the control of the Barren County railroad was completed, in 1871 the Memphis branch was completed and was operated in connection with the Memphis, Clarksville, & Louisville and the Memphis & Ohio Railroads. On May 4, 1871, the Nashville & Decatur Railroad was leased to the L&N. On October 1, 1872, the South & North Alabama Railroad was completed. The L&N purchased the Cumberland & Ohio Railroad, which ran from Lebanon to Greensburg and was completed in 1879. In 1879, the company also bought the Tennessee division of the St. Louis & Southwestern Railroad and the Kentucky division of the same railroad.[96]

The L&N purchased the majority of stocks in other railroads, such as the Nashville, Chattanooga & St. Louis Railway system, the Owensboro & Nashville Railroad and the Mobile & Montgomery Railroad. It leased the New Orleans & Mobile Railroad and the Pontchartrain Railroad. It also leased the Southern division of the Cumberland & Ohio Railroad, the Indiana and Illinois division of the St. Louis and Southeastern Railroad and the Selma division of the Western Railroad of Alabama. The L&N also purchased the Pensacola Railroad and the Pensacola & Selma Railroad. In 1885, the L&N had control of 2,027 miles of track and transported 569,149 people. The man most responsible for the expansion of the L&N Railroad was Victor Newcomb.[97]

Union Station
1000 West Broadway

The railroad station was opened on September 7, 1891, by the Louisville and Nashville Railroad. The station succeeded previous, smaller depots around Louisville at the time. Completed in 1889 at a cost of over $310,000, the facility was once the largest railroad station in the southern U.S., covering forty acres.

Designed by F.W. Mobray in the Richardsonian Romanesque style, the station's brick-faced limestone ashlar was quarried in Bowling Green, Kentucky, and the Bedford stone trim was from Indiana. The roof, trussed with a combination of heavy wood and iron, is covered with slate. Architectural features include a clock tower, smaller towers, turrets, a façade of considerable size and barreled

Union Station, 1000 West Broadway. *Courtesy of the author.*

vaulting. The interior featured an atrium, dining and spacious ladies' retiring rooms on the first floor. A wrought-iron balcony overlooks the atrium. Soft lighting comes from rose-colored windows on both sides of the atrium. The walls are made of marble from Georgia, as well as oak and southern pine. Ceramic tile covers the floor. In 1905, a fire occurred in the facility, and the original rose-colored windows were replaced with an eighty-four-panel stained-glass skylight that became a feature of the barrel-vaulting tower. At the height of rail travel in the 1920s, the station served fifty-eight trains a day. The popularity of rail travel had diminished by the mid-1960s. Amtrak used the facility from 1971 until 1976, when the passenger company began running the Floridian in conjunction with the Auto-Train from a suburban station. From 2001 to 2003, a track on the west side of the parking lot served Amtrak's Kentucky Cardinal to Chicago. In 1980, the Louisville & Nashville Railroad sold the station to the Transit Authority of River City and currently serves as its administrative offices. The first floor is open to the public from 8:00 a.m. to 5:00 p.m., Monday through Friday.[98]

The first president of the Louisville and Nashville Railroad was L.L. Shreve, who was appointed by the board of directors on September 27, 1851, and resigned in 1854. In 1884, the president of the railroad was Milton H. Smith. Over twelve thousand men were employed by the company, and the capital stock in 1885 was $30 million.[99]

The Louisville, New Albany & Chicago Railroad main line ran from New Albany to Michigan City for 228 miles. Its branch, the Chicago & Indianapolis Airline, which ran from Indianapolis to Chicago for 176 miles, connected the two cities by the short line and connected with the Monon, Indiana line. The railroad was founded on January 25, 1847, and opened in 1852.[100]

The Jeffersonville, Madison, and Indianapolis Railroad ran from north of the city, crossed the Ohio and Mississippi Railway at Seymour, Indiana, formed a junction with the Madison branch at Columbus and connected with Indianapolis with 110 miles. The Pennsylvania Company also operated the Shelby and Rush Railroad and the Cambridge Extension for a total of 225 miles.[101]

The Ohio and Mississippi Railroad connected with Louisville with a branch in North Vernon, Indiana. The Louisville branch ran from North Vernon to Jeffersonville with fifty-two miles. The Ohio and Mississippi ran from Cincinnati to St. Louis and their Springfield division ran from Shawneetown to Bardstown, Illinois, for a total of 615,000 miles. The railroad was completed in 1867 and built by two corporations.[102]

The Chesapeake, Ohio & Southwestern started from Richmond, Virginia, and ran to Huntington, West Virginia. From Huntington, the railroad was constructed to Mount Sterling, Kentucky, where the line connected with the Louisville, Cincinnati and Lexington Railroad. The Chesapeake, Ohio & Southwestern Railroad was completed in 1881 and formed the most direct route between the Eastern Seaboard and the West. The railroad supplied coal, iron and timber. The railroad company also bought the Elizabethtown and Paducah Railroad, which established a connection with the Iron Mountain Railroad at Cairo, Illinois. With this connection, Louisville was open to trade with the entire Southwest and to the sea. The owners of the Chesapeake, Ohio & Southwestern Railroad were also owners of the Western division of the Southern Pacific Railroad and made their railroad the eastern or Atlantic division of the inter-oceanic system of the South. The arrangement boosted Louisville as an important railroad center.[103]

The Louisville, New Albany, and St. Louis Railway gave Louisville the most direct line from the West and a connection with the Missouri Pacific, Union and Central Pacific railways, together with the Chesapeake, Ohio & Southwestern.[104]

The Louisville Southern Railroad gave Louisville a direct southern route, along with the Danville and the Cincinnati Southern to Chattanooga, placing Louisville in immediate connection with the southern Atlantic seacoast through a railroad system centering at, and extending east and south through, Virginia, Georgia and Alabama. Ex-Colonel Bennett Young was the founder of the Indiana and Kentucky Bridge and also founder of the Louisville Southern Railroad.[105]

Streetcar railways were intricately tied to the rise of manufacturing. They provided the necessary transportation for workers who had to live on the outskirts of the city where new housing could be built inexpensively. General Jeremiah Boyle, a Union general during the Civil War, founded the Louisville City Railway, of which he was president. He ran a franchise to operate streetcar lines on Main Street and other thoroughfares. At Twelfth Street, the City Railway connected with the old Louisville & Portland. Boyle secured a parallel route on Portland Avenue. He eventually extended his lines on Preston to Lion Garden at St. Catherine, on Second Street to Breckinridge and on Broadway to Cave Hill Cemetery. The Central Passenger Railway built lines on Fourth Street to Oak Street and to Walnut between Eighteenth and Baxter. The Citizen's Passenger Railway ran lines on Market between Twentieth and Woodlawn Garden at the east end of Market Street. The Beargrass line had routes from Bardstown Turnpike to Doup's Point, then along the Taylorsville Turnpike to the area of Bowman Field. By the 1870s, fifty miles of streetcar lines carried eight million passengers a year.[106]

Louisville had a great supply of real estate. The city was built at the northern edge of a plain covering 70 or 80 square miles. The corporate limits of the city included about 12.5 square miles with 144 miles of paved streets. There were 124 miles of horse, steam and suburban railways. The street railway lines had a fixed fare of five cents and a system of transfers that helped build up the suburbs and relieved the pressure on the city. The streetcar system resulted in making desirable property cheaper for manufactories, residences and business houses. By 1889, the electric trolley car replaced the older mule-drawn cars. By 1890, all the local lines merged into the Louisville Railway Company. The new company set about to convert the major routes to electric operation.[107]

In 1880, the value of land was assessed at $27,149,665; by 1887, the value had increased to $31,550,000. The homes in Louisville were cheap, workshops were taxed lightly and the buildings that businesses rented had a fair market rental price. The low cost of real estate, the proximity of raw materials and fuel and the increase of railroad lines were the main factors that contributed to Louisville becoming a major industrial city. "Shotgun" cottages, a style borrowed from New Orleans, were built for the working class on the outskirts of the city. Each cottage had a narrow lot of land.[108] While the population of the city increased 25 percent from 1870 to 1880, from 1880 to 1886, the population increased about 40 percent, but industries increased 90 percent. The resident population was being used in manufacturing companies, which led to skilled and educated mechanics.[109]

With the newfound prosperity in Louisville, wealthy industrialists and financiers gave a substantial amount of their wealth to improving the city. For example, in 1887, tan-leather business owner Colonel Andrew Cowan sent a proposal to the Salmagundi Club to fund a system of parks and wanted the business community to support the effort. In 1890, the Board of Park Commissioners was empowered to select land to build the new park system. Iroquois Park was the first park to be planned, with a Grand Boulevard, which would later become Southern Parkway, that connected a road from downtown to the southwest. Eventually, Southern, Eastern and Western parkways connected all the parks. Cherokee Park in the east end was purchased in 1891; Shawnee Park in the west end was bought a year later. Frederick Law Olmstead designed the new park system, with landscapes, road systems and planting patterns. The arrival of the electric trolley and the parks created a boom in real estate.[110]

During the Gilded Age in Louisville, as there was an abundance of wealth, residents could indulge in the new outlets for entertainment. The Masonic Temple on Fourth Avenue and Jefferson Street hosted Oscar Wilde and Mark Twain. In 1873, Macauley's Theater opened on Walnut Street near Fourth Avenue. This is where Mary Anderson gave her infrequent Louisville appearances. Macauley's Theater gave Louisville residents performances of Shakespeare and Buffalo Bill. In 1883, it hosted the American premiere of Henrik Ibsen's masterpiece *A Doll's House*, with Helen Modjeska in the title role. The Liederkranz Hall, built by the Liederkranz Society, was used by touring opera companies and by German-language theatrical troupes. The Buckingham, owned by brothers John and James Whallen, opened in Louisville. They presented vaudeville and burlesque shows. The Whallens also opened the Grand Opera House on the north side of Jefferson Street between Second and Third, only a block from the Buckingham. In 1898, the Buckingham was moved to the Grand Opera House. There was also the Harris Museum on Fourth Avenue.[111] In 1874, Churchill Downs was organized as the Louisville Jockey Club and Driving Park Association. Its first president was Meriwether Lewis Clark Jr. The Kentucky Derby was the showpiece of the new approach to horse racing. A $1,000 purse was given to the winner of the three-year-olds. On opening day, May 17, 1875, over ten thousand people attended the new track. It was the largest crowd for any opening of a new track or the first running of a new stakes race.

Churchill Downs
700 Central Avenue

Meriwether Lewis Clark Jr., the grandson of William Clark of the Lewis and Clark Expedition, founded Churchill Downs in 1875. The first race occurred on May 17, 1875. In 1872, Clark traveled to London and France and attended the Epsom Derby in England, which led to his idea to import the race to Louisville. The track was built on 80 acres of land that Clark leased from his uncles John and Henry Churchill. He also built a clubhouse and grandstand. Clark started with three major stakes: the Kentucky Derby, the Kentucky Oaks and the Clark Handicap. The races were modeled after three premier races in England. The winner of the first race was Bonaventure, but the first Kentucky Derby winner was Aristides. Aristides was trained and ridden by two African Americans, Ansel

Churchill Downs, located at 700 Central Avenue. *Courtesy of Steve Wiser.*

Williamson and Oliver Lewis. Today, Churchill Downs encompasses 147 acres and recently underwent a major renovation, including a huge screen to watch the races. Churchill Downs owns the record for the longest-running, continuous sporting event in the United States.[112] In 1985, Churchill Downs opened the Kentucky Derby Museum, which includes a multi-projector presentation.

In 1889, William F. Norton Jr. built the Auditorium at Fourth and Hill. It could seat three thousand people. The back of the Auditorium also had an outdoor amphitheater. He held fireworks displays with the *Burning of Moscow* and *The Last Days of Pompeii*. He also held bicycle races and other outdoor events. Norton brought musicians and singers to Louisville from New York and Boston symphonies, the Metropolitan Opera, and Edward Strauss's orchestra from Vienna. The venue hosted regular seasons of opera, including works by Gilbert and Sullivan. The Auditorium also was the home of drama; the great names of nineteenth-century stage appeared, including Ellen Terry, Sarah Bernhardt, Lillian Russell, Nat Goodwin, Edwin Booth and Lawrence Barrett.[113]

With the influx of newfound wealth, Louisville residents could support the arts community. Carl Brenner was known for his landscapes, and Nicola Marschall, who designed the Confederate uniform and Confederate flag during the Civil War, was a portrait artist who moved to Louisville after the war. Aurelius O. Revenaugh was also a portrait artist in the city. Patty Thum was a female artist whose work was showcased at the Southern Exposition. Native Louisville resident Enid Yandell, who studied art under Auguste Rodin, did work on the exterior decoration of the Women's Building at Chicago's Columbian Exposition. She later did the statue of Daniel Boone and Hogan's Fountain at Cherokee Park and the figures for Louisville's Confederate monument, now located in Brandenburg, Kentucky.[114]

Simmons College
1018 South Seventh Street

On November 25, 1879, the Kentucky Normal and Theological Institute became the first African American–controlled higher education institution in Kentucky. In November of that year, the

Simmons College, 1018 South Seventh Street. *Courtesy of Steve Wiser.*

Convention of Colored Baptists Church in Kentucky purchased four acres of land on the corner of Seventh and Kentucky Streets for the campus. The college was headed by Reverend Elijah P. Marrs. In September 1880, the General Association of Colored Baptists of Kentucky hired Reverend William J. Simmons as president. In 1885, the college was renamed State University. Simmons resigned in 1890. In 1918, Reverend Charles H. Parrish Sr. was appointed president and changed the name to Simmons College. On August 31, 1931, the University of Louisville purchased Simmons College for the future location of the Louisville Municipal College for African Americans. In 1934, the University of Louisville bought the remaining property at Simmons College, and the name of the school was changed Simmons Bible College. It was moved to Eighteenth and Dumesnil Streets. In 2005, Dr. Kevin W. Cosby became the thirteenth president of the school and changed the name to Simmons College of Kentucky. In 2006, the college moved back to its original campus on Seventh Street. The institution is the nation's 107th historically Black college.[115]

During the Gilded Age, Louisville saw an explosion in banks, stores, drugstores, hotels, merchant shops and factories. The number of banks increased from 3 in 1819 to 29 in 1883, and by the turn of the century, Louisville had the largest banking capital in the South. The number of wholesale and retail stores increased from 36 in 1819 to 1,555 in 1883; commission stores increased from 14 in 1819 to 60 in 1883. The number of bookstores increased from 3 to 29 in 1883; printing offices increased from

3 to 39; and drugstores increased from 3 to 93. In addition, the number of hotels and taverns increased from 6 to 32; groceries increased from 28 to 786; merchant shops of all kinds increased from 64 to 1,109; steam factories and mills increased from 3 to 487; and different types of factories increased from 11 to 515.[116]

To showcase the rising importance of manufacturing, on September 3, 1872, the city opened a Louisville Industrial Exposition, which ran annually through 1882, except for 1876, when the United States hosted the Centennial Exposition in Philadelphia. A building was constructed on the northeast corner of Fourth and Chestnut. The exposition showcased the city's manufacturers, who displayed their products for sale to potential buyers. The directors of the exposition were the city's top industrialists, including foundry men J.H. Wramplemeier, Charles Snead and George Ainsle, papermaker and railroad promoter Biderman Dupont and railroad financier H. Victor Newcomb. John T. Moore was the president of the exposition. He was a paper manufacturer and wholesale grocer. In 1877, at the Louisville Industrial Exposition was the telephone, invented by Alexander Graham Bell. In 1879, the American District Telegraph Company brought the telephone into Louisville homes and businesses. James Breckinridge Speed was president of the company. Speed was already president of another of the city's industrial markets, the Louisville Cement Company.[117]

Another highlight of the Industrial Exposition was the electric light bulb. In 1878, arc lights were installed in William Kelly's axe factory on Portland Avenue and in James Lithgow's Eagle Foundry at Main and Clay. Five years later, at the Southern Exposition, which opened its doors in 1883 and ran until 1887, the electric incandescent light bulb, invented by Thomas Edison, was featured. The Southern Exposition showcased agricultural machinery and technical innovations. With over 1,500 commercial and mercantile attractions, the Southern Exposition exhibited its wares, hoping for buyers. Over 4,600 incandescent light bulbs were installed at the Southern Exposition Building. The exposition was Louisville's single most ambitious promotional effort. It was financed completely with local private capital.[118]

The massive foundries and mills in Louisville were fueled by coal and coke. The city became a distribution point for southbound coal, both by river and rail. In 1887, about $3 million of Pittsburgh coal was handled in the Louisville harbor annually, with about two-thirds going downstream. The coal was distributed all along the Ohio River and the upper and lower Mississippi, with over ten million tons annually reaching New Orleans and the lower coast. The L&N also brought in coal to Louisville from the Jellico and Laurel mines.[119]

Banks were needed to fund the immense commerce and trade in Louisville. There were twenty-nine banks in Louisville in 1883: the Bank of Kentucky, the Bank of Louisville, the Bank of Commerce, the Falls City Bank, Farmers and Drovers Banks, German Bank, German Insurance Bank, German Security Bank, Louisville Banking Company, Masonic Bank, People's Bank, Western Bank, First National Bank, Second National Bank, Third National Bank, Fourth National Bank, Citizen's National Bank, German National Bank, Kentucky National Bank, Louisville City National Bank and Merchants National Bank. The banks had a combined capital of $9,201,800, with a surplus of $2,565,279. From April to September 1887, 50 new manufacturing companies were built in Louisville. Also in that period, there were 1,400 new buildings erected at a cost of $4,000,000.[120] The following establishments opened in the 1870s: the Louisville Public Library (1872), the new Louisville City Hall (1873), the Alms House (1874) and the Louisville Clearing House (1875). In 1878, the following establishments opened: the Louisville College of Pharmacy and the American Printing House of the Blind (both on October 8), the Masonic Widows and Orphans Home (October 24) and the Masonic Grand Lodge (October 25).[121]

American Printing House for the Blind
1839 Frankfort Avenue

In 1854, Morrison Heady collected donations so he could print a raised-letter version of Milton's *Paradise Lost.* Two years later, Heady inspired Dempsey B. Sherrod, a blind man, to raise funds in his state of Mississippi. Sherrod's idea was to establish a national printing house for raised-print books. In 1858, the Mississippi legislature, along with Sherrod, established the American Printing House for the Blind. The Kentucky General Assembly passed an act establishing the company, and space was set aside for the Kentucky Institution for the Education of the Blind. In 1879, the U.S. Congress passed an act that provided a subsidy to the American Printing House for the Blind. Congress established a perpetual fund to be spent annually on the manufacture of books and other materials for the blind. The books and materials are distributed free

American Printing House for the Blind, 1839 Frankfort Avenue. *Courtesy of Michael Hudson, American Printing House for the Blind.*

A child exploring the American Printing House for the Blind Museum. *Courtesy of Michael Hudson, American Printing House for the Blind.*

Early Clamshells Printers at the American Printing House for the Blind. *Courtesy of Michael Hudson, American Printing House for the Blind.*

of charge to students at state residential schools for the blind. Today, the American Printing House for the Blind is the oldest company in the United States manufacturing products for blind and visually impaired people. It is also the world's largest. The company is also a leading distributor of software that makes computers accessible to the blind.[122]

In 1880, Durkee Famous Foods, Theodore Tafel Surgical Instrument Company and Ballard and Ballard Flour Mill opened. In 1881, the Kentucky Elevator Company was founded. In 1882, the Louisville Electric Light Company opened. The following year, the Ohio Valley Telephone company opened. The following establishments were founded in 1887: the Astoria Veneer Mills and Lumber Company, J.F. Kurfees Paint Company, the Seelbach "European Style" hotel and the Frey Planning Mill Company.[123]

The Seelbach Hotel
500 Fourth Street

In 1869, two Bavarian brothers, Louis and Otto Seelbach, moved to Louisville to learn the hotel business. By 1903, after several years of running restaurants and gentleman's clubs, the brothers began construction of a new hotel at the corner of Fourth and Walnut Streets. In May 1905, Seelbach Hotel celebrated its grand opening, drawing 25,000 visitors to its five-hour public inspection. Designed by W.J. Dodd of Louisville and F.M. Andrews of Dayton, Ohio, the Seelbach boasts a lavish turn-of-the century Beaux-Arts baroque architectural style, embodying the old-world opulence of Viennese and Parisian hotels. Equally grand, the hotel interiors feature a lobby furnished with combined marbles from Italy, Vermont and Switzerland along with mahogany and bronze in a classic Renaissance style, and a vaulted dome of eight hundred glass panes. Arthur Thomas, the most famous Indian painter in

This page and following two pages: Seelbach Hotel, located at 500 Fourth Street. *Courtesy of Jim Meyer, director of sales and marketing, Seelbach Hotel.*

the world, was commissioned to decorate the lobby with huge mural paintings of pioneer scenes from Kentucky history. During Prohibition, gangsters such as Lucky Luciano, "Beer Baron of the Bronx" Dutch Schultz and Al Capone visited the hotel. Capone frequented the Seelbach, and his legacy remains in the Oakroom restaurant, where guests can dine in the small alcove where he played cards. The gangster's favorite room has two hidden doors behind special panels, leading to secret passageways, and it still displays the large mirror Capone sent from Chicago so that he could watch his back. In 1925, F. Scott Fitzgerald immortalized George Remus, known as the "King of the Bootleggers," and the hotel in his novel *The Great Gatsby*. Remus was the inspiration for the novel's title character, Jay Gatsby, and Fitzgerald referred to the Seelbach and the hotel's Grand Ballroom when characters Tom Buchanan and Daisy were married in Louisville.[124]

In 1889, Gould-Levy Broomworks opened. In 1891, the J.C. Heitzman Bakery, Ohio River Stone Company and J.J. Mueller Tailoring Company opened. In 1893, R.C. Schlich & H.C. Kottke Company and William Mayer established the first commercial photo-engraving business in the city. These businesses were a small fraction of the buildings that rose across the city during the Gilded Age.[125]

Two of the leading industries in Louisville during the Gilded Age were whiskey and tobacco. The American Industrial Revolution changed the bourbon industry at this time and transformed the spirit from a product of small-batch production to the bourbon that Americans know today. Whiskey-bourbon became the leading industrial product in the state. Several areas in Kentucky claimed the first manufacture of whiskey. Mason County claimed that the state's first distillery was located a few miles from the present town of Maysville. Nelson County also claimed to be the first location of a distillery. Mercer County claimed that the first distillery was built in Harrodsburg, the earliest permanent settlement in Kentucky. General James Wilkinson was the owner and operator of the distillery, but he did not arrive in Kentucky until 1784. In 1783, Evan Williams built and operated a still at the corner of Fifth and Water Streets in the settlement of Louisville, at the Falls of the Ohio. He used the abundant supply of corn to make his whiskey. He was Kentucky's first commercial distiller but also a member of the Board of Trustees of Louisville. Before he became a member of the board, a rule had been adopted forbidding liquor during the meetings under penalty of censure and the chairman was to instantly "remove" the liquor. If the violator was caught a second time bringing liquor to a meeting, a fine of six shillings would be collected from the violator; the liquor was to be seized and used by the board after adjournment of the meeting. Williams did not know about the rule and brought a bottle of his own whiskey to the meeting for the refreshment of his fellow members. The members seized his liquor but without censure. At the end of the meeting, Williams left with an empty bottle. At the next meeting, he brought another bottle, but Will Johnson, the county clerk, declared that Williams ought to be expelled for making and offering to the board his whiskey. The clerk was also surveyor of the port and was accustomed to the use of imported wines and liquors. In his defense, Williams insisted that the clerk had the taste of an aristocrat; the board agreed with him, and again Williams left with an empty bottle without censure. He continued to make his whiskey without license until 1788, when he was forced to pay his license. He continued to run his distillery.[126] In the 1780s, James Spears, a distiller from Paris, Kentucky, first used the term *bourbon*.

In 1787, a great boost in the manufacture of whiskey in Kentucky arose when a colony of immigrants from Maryland arrived in Kentucky. They were known as the "Catholic League." Sixty families came down the Ohio River in flatboats and settled in Nelson, Washington and Marion Counties. They brought with them the knowledge of distilling and established early distilleries along the Salt River, down which they sent their product to the settlements and cities of the Ohio and Mississippi Rivers. Nelson County possessed an abundant supply of limestone water. It was and remains the principal center for distilleries in Kentucky and made the finest whiskies in the state.[127]

Elijah Craig was credited with being the first distiller to age his whiskey in charred oak barrels. No one knows how Elijah began charring his barrels. Once he began using the barrels, the whiskey changed into an amber color, with a distinctive flavor that makes what we now know today as bourbon. Many consider Elijah Craig the father of bourbon.[128]

In 1791, an excise law was passed by Congress for the purpose of raising federal revenue. The distillers in Pennsylvania opposed the tax and, in 1794, openly opposed the tax. President George Washington told the insurgents to disperse and warned the people not to resist the federal government. The militia was called out and directed to quell the rebellion. The insurgents to the tax law backed down, and General Harry Lee issued a proclamation granting amnesty to all who had submitted to the laws. The insurgents had to take the oath of allegiance. The insurgence was known as the Whiskey Rebellion of Pennsylvania. With the law passed, many of the distillers in Pennsylvania moved to Kentucky, settling in Mason County. The government of Kentucky did not interfere with the distillers, who were able to convert their corn into whiskey without a tax. Kentucky whiskey occupied the pioneers of the state. Whiskey became a form of exchange and a standard of value. The product was in universal demand and did not deteriorate but actually improved with age. The product could be easily transported and could be disposed of in any town or city along the Ohio or Mississippi Rivers. Settlements of accounts were made in whiskey, and many professional men received their wages in whiskey.[129]

In 1794, Alexander Anderson of Philadelphia introduced the perpetual steam still. By 1801, whiskey and tobacco had replaced flour as the principal export crop from Kentucky's interior, with 56,000 gallons traveling down the Ohio River and passing through the Louisville Customs House. By 1810, 250,000 gallons of whiskey were being transported down the Ohio River; by 1822, that total was 2,250,000.[130] By 1815, the steam-powered perpetual still was being used as far west as Kentucky; by 1818, it had replaced the copper still that George Washington and Evan Williams would have used in their whiskey production. By 1830, Aeneas Coffey invented the column still, an advanced variant of the Alexander Anderson perpetual still. Coffey's still could produce 3,000 gallons of raw whiskey in an hour.[131]

Scotland native James Crow studied medicine and chemistry at Edinburg University. In 1823, he immigrated to Kentucky and opened his own distilleries, including Glenn's Creek Distillery and later Old Oscar Pepper Distillery. He applied the scientific method to distilling. He used saccharimeters to gauge the sugar content of the mash and thermometers to regulate the mash's temperature and took careful measurements of acidity levels throughout the process. His contribution to the history of the sour mash process for regulatory batch consistency was the addition of a small quantity of leftover mash (the mixture of grain, malt, water and yeast) from the previous batch. In adding a small amount of the previous mash to the current mash, he was able to regulate the PH levels in each run of the still, enabling consistency on a large scale.[132]

The invention of bigger and more efficient stills and James Crow's invention of palatable bourbon helped to produce a quality product on a large scale, but whiskey-bourbon went into decline, and by 1846, there were no distilleries in Louisville. In 1821, the Hope Distillery turned out one thousand gallons of whiskey, but the company was a failure because it ran out of people to drink the product. Steam power, modern buildings, advanced machinery and high-volume stills helped with production, but once made, the whiskey-bourbon could only be delivered by either wagon or steam-powered boats, which could take months to deliver the product to the East Coast or New Orleans.[133]

After the Civil War, the production of whiskey made a comeback. Railroads changed how bourbon was delivered. By 1865, there were 35,000 miles of track. By 1870, 53,000 miles of track had been laid. The numbers continued to increase. By 1880, there were 93,000 miles of track, and by 1890, the total had reached 164,000 miles. As mentioned previously, when the Louisville and Nashville Railroad connected with other railroads, the trains could reach all corners of the nation delivering bourbon to the entire country and even overseas via steam-powered ocean liners. The Industrial Revolution also changed the farm with modern equipment, such as Avery's plows and artificial fertilizers. Annual corn production in 1860 was 838.8 million bushels, but by 1900, corn production had risen to 2.7 billion bushels. More corn meant more whiskey and, hence, more bourbon.[134] But with the gilded lining, major corporations took over the small stills and turned the business of bourbon into a multimillion-dollar industry. The building of bonded warehouses, the knowledge of intricate laws and rulings and the great expense essential to compliance with all the demands of the government, together with the capital required to meet the taxes as they matured, had the effect of gradually replacing the farmer who made whiskey on a small scale and put the manufacturing of the product in the hands of corporations and individuals with strong financial resources. The bourbon industry was almost ruined by deceptive practices, such as adding flavoring or colors to bourbon to mask the inferior quality. The master distillers in Kentucky took back their product and demanded regulations. Batches were tested and bourbon was bottled with bonded labels to make sure the product was not tampered with. Government regulations made sure that what was in the bottle actually was bourbon.

In 1880, Kentucky saw 15,011,279 gallons of whiskey produced; by 1895, that number had increased to 22,814,950. Kentucky distillers spent millions of dollars per year in the purchase of grain, fuel, barrels and machinery, as well as for labor, insurance and transportation. In 1895, there were nineteen distillers in Louisville, plus additional distillers in Nelson, Davies and Anderson Counties, which added to the output of bourbon manufacturing. Several of the distilleries had the warehouse capacity for more than one hundred thousand barrels of whiskey. The production of and trade in fine bourbons was one of the greatest industries in Kentucky and took up a large amount of capital in Louisville. The city was the collection center and contained one hundred registered grain distilleries. The production capacity was 82,000 gallons per day. The gross product during the five years ending in June 1887 was 35,000 gallons, with internal revenue taxes amounting to $29,154,319.[135] By 1904, 436,013 barrels were shipped from Louisville, which converts to 21,000,000 gallons of whiskey-bourbon. Louisville handled one-sixth of the total consumption of the United States and was the largest market for fine whiskey in the nation. The value of the shipments was $36,991,040. The total production of whiskey-bourbon in the state of Kentucky for 1904 was 23,070,162 gallons, of which 11,398,394 gallons were produced in Louisville. By the turn of the century, Louisville led the world in whiskey-bourbon.[136]

The following were some of the distillers in Louisville: J.M. Mattingly & Sons, located on High Avenue in Portland and office on 205 West Main Street; Block, Franck & Company (205 West Main); J.B. Wathen & Brothers Company (141 West Main Street); Anderson & Nelson Distilleries Company (116 East Main Street); Applegate & Sons (122 East Main Street); Parkland Distillery Company (126 East Main Street); Hollenback & Vetter, owner of the Glencoe Distillery (234 Second Street); Ashton Distillery Company (120 East Main); John Roach, maker of "Old Times" (104 East Main Street); J.H. Cutter, maker of Old Bourbon; C.P. Moorman & Company (104 East Main Street); Marion County Distillery (Thirty-First Street and Rudd Avenue); and J.M. Atherton Company (125 West Main Street).[137]

Whiskey Row
101–133 West Main Street

The stretch of Renaissance Revival buildings located along Main Street is known as Whiskey Row (also known as the Iron Quarter) and is the birthplace of bourbon. The block once served as home of the bourbon industry in Louisville. The cast-iron storefronts were built between 1850 and 1905. The building at 105 West Main Street was erected in 1877 and designed by Henry Whitestone. It housed the business of W.H. Thomas and Son, a wholesale whiskey dealership. In 1895, the building was taken over by J.T.S. Brown

This page: Whiskey Row, located at 101–133 West Main Street. *Courtesy of the author.*

Evan Williams Bourbon Experience, located at 528 West Main Street, "Whiskey Row." *Courtesy of Steve Wiser.*

and Sons, predecessor of the Brown-Forman Corporation. The structures at 107–109 West Main Street were built in 1905 and designed by Dennis Xavier Murphy for J.T.S. Brown and Sons. The building was later occupied by the wholesale grocery company Bolinger-Babbage & Company. The building at 111 West Main Street, erected in 1871, was a pork-packing company and woolen mill. Later, the building was a warehouse for the Bacon's Department Store. The structures at 111–115 West Main Street was built in 1857 and served as the main offices and salesroom for the Belknap Hardware and Manufacturing Company from 1881 to 1924. At one time, the Belknap company was the largest hardware firm in the country. The building at 117 West Main was constructed in 1857 and held pork dealers and brokers. The building at 119 West Main Street, erected in 1860, originally housed pork dealers, but in 1895, it was purchased by whiskey dealer Samuel Grabfelder and Company.[138] In 2010, Whiskey Row Historic District was listed in the National Register of Historic Places. Today, Whiskey Row has revitalized its connection with bourbon. Tourists can visit the Evan Williams Bourbon Experience and Old Forrester Distillery. Whiskey Row also has O'Sheay's Restaurant and Duluth's Trading Company. Louisville residents can live at the Whiskey Row Lofts. Near Whiskey Row is Angel's Envy, the Jim Beam Urban Stillhouse, Kentucky Peerless and Rabbit Hole Distillery.

During the Gilded Age, Louisville was the world's largest tobacco market, tobacco re-handler and tobacco manufacturer. The state of Kentucky produced almost 50 percent of the American crop. Louisville was the chief dealer in tobacco. One-third of all tobacco raised in North America was handled in the warehouses of Louisville in 1885 and 1886. The city's great importance as a tobacco market was because it was the only city in the United States where all grades could be obtained. Tobacco became an early feature in Kentucky's culture. The settlers from Virginia were tobacco planters, and tobacco was one of the first crops grown in the state. The settlers who moved to Kentucky arrived in 1775; eight years later, the crop had become an important staple. Kentucky built warehouses for storing and inspecting tobacco. One was located on the land of Colonel John Campbell in Louisville; another was at the mouth of Hickman's Creek on the Kentucky River. A third warehouse was located at Leestown, just below Frankfort. Campbell erected a warehouse in Shippingport and another on Beargrass Creek.[139]

Tobacco could be easily transported by flatboat and demanded a cash sale. Tobacco was a legal tender for the payment of debts under the laws of Virginia. On June 28, 1794, the Virginia Laws were repealed when it came to payment of tobacco for court fees. In 1810, cultivation of the crop began in Logan County. By 1820, a number of planters began to grow crops in that area. In Green, Barren, Hardin and Warren Counties, the cultivation of the crop began about the same time as at Logan.

The foreign trade of tobacco became important, and companies arose to strip the tobacco and make cigars, snuff and chewing tobacco. Elisha Applegate was the first tobacco dealer in Louisville. He was born on March 25, 1782. He handled and sold tobacco for forty years. In 1835, there was only one warehouse, located on Seventh and Main Streets. In 1844, a second warehouse was built by Joshua Haynes and John Rowzee (Floyd and Preston Streets). In 1851, George Green and Thomas Rowland built the Farmer's warehouse (Second between Main and the river). Another facility was built by Page & Ronald on Main Street and also called the Farmer's warehouse. In 1851, the Pickett warehouse was built. The proprietors were Joshua Haynes and Andrew Graham. Graham became one of the most noted and daring speculators in tobacco. The warehouse was named after James Pickett, a pioneer warehouseman.

Trade amounted to ten thousand to twelve thousand hogsheads of tobacco a year. In 1855, a commission house was built on Ninth Street. John Brent and Frank Ronald were the owners. In 1861, the Boone warehouse was built, owned by Captain William Glover. In 1863, the reopening of the Louisville House took place. Its owner was James Phelps. His sons operated the Planters warehouse.

In 1870, Page and Company built Farmers warehouse, which was not to be confused with the earlier Page & Ronald warehouse. In 1895, there were eighteen warehouses, including Pickett, Ninth Street, Louisville, Planter's, Green River, Grinter & Company, Farmer's, Fall City, Growers', New Enterprise, Brown, Tate & Company, Rice & Givens, Central, Golden Rule, Eagle, Major and Owen. Besides the Civil War, the factor that had the greatest influence on the tobacco market was the revitalization of burley tobacco. Burley, one of the most profitable crops that could be grown, was raised in the Bluegrass region of Kentucky. Pastures once used for the raising of Thoroughbreds were now plowed up to raise Burley tobacco. The tobacco merchants in Louisville met with Milton Smith, the president of the Louisville and Nashville Railroad, and stated their case. Smith readjusted the tariff on tobacco, and the railroad cooperated with the transports on the Kentucky River in bringing Louisville the Burley tobacco from the fields.[140]

In 1850, Louisville sold 7,500 hogsheads of tobacco, and by 1895, the city had sold 174,885 hogsheads. In 1889, there were 61,641 planters of tobacco, 274,587 acres were devoted to the crop and the value on the farms was $13,155,297. In 1895, Kentucky ranked third in the number of establishments devoted to the making of chewing and smoking tobacco and snuff, fifth in the amount of capital invested and third in the value of wages paid. The state was fourth in the number of employees, fourth in the value of raw material used and third in value of the finished product.

The state had a growing industry in making cigars. In 1879, there were 144 businesses engaged in the industry, with a capital of $528,297, annual wages of $375,259 and a total product value of $1,058,039. In 1894, the number of cigars made in the 295 factories in the state was 42,026,065. Of these cigars, 14,364,040 were made in Louisville. Chewing tobacco, plug and fine cut amounted to 18,074,640 pounds for Louisville alone.[141]

R.N. Edwell & Company, located on 129 Third Street, owned the Louisville cigar factory. R.P. Gregory manufactured cigars. The Franklin Tobacco Company (633 and 635 East Main Street) manufactured half dime, gingerbread nip and chewing tobacco. Jacob Dautrich (1405 Shelby Street) made cigar boxes.

On January 7, 1889, Nick Finzer was president of the Leaf Tobacco Exchange, which was made up of both buyers and warehousemen. The exchange replaced the Tobacco Board of Trade and the Louisville Leaf Tobacco Buyer's Association. In 1885, the buyer's association was dissolved. On February 12, 1876, the board of trade was organized by the buyers and warehousemen. By 1895, each was their own separate organization, but the exchange was the principal body, and J.S. Bockee was president.

Louisville had the reputation as one of the leading tobacco plug centers in the world. The Finzers, the Doerhoefers, the Weissingers and the Matthewses built immense factories that employed thousands of workers. The American Tobacco Company was important in the manufacture of chewing tobacco. John Doerhoefer was made director of the company, and Louisville became the base from which most of the tobacco supplies were drawn and was the center of plug tobacco.

The buyers formed another important element of the tobacco trade. Many were agents of foreign government monopolies. Others bought and sold on their own, and still others acted as brokers for manufacturers or exporters. James Clark, Daniel Spalding, W.G. Meier, Anderson Burge and many others were connected as buyers. Historic firms from Liverpool, London, Bremen and Antwerp had resident agents. In addition, resident agents for the government monopolies of France, Spain and Italy were in the city.

Tobacco was sold in hogsheads, or wooden casks. The staves of the cask are lifted off, and the mass is broken into three points, from which samples are drawn. The samples are taken from any point in the hogshead and are meant to represent the quality of the entire cask. When the sample "hands" are drawn, an inspector stamps them with an official seal as a guarantee that the whole will meet these specimens. The buyer examines the samples and bids. The breaking of the hogsheads to draw samples is known as "the breaks."[142]

During the Gilded Age, Louisville was the largest market in the United States and the largest market in the world for jeans and jeans clothing. In 1880, there were four large mills engaged, accounting for about $1,120,000 worth of capital, using 1,250 employees and producing annually nearly 7,500,000 yards of cloth, valued at $2,250,000. In 1887, the capacity of the industry increased 20 percent. In just ten years, the industry increased eightfold.[143]

Conrad-Caldwell House
1402 St. James Court

The Conrad-Caldwell House Museum is a Victorian mansion located in the heart of Old Louisville on St. James Court. The home is one of the finest examples of Richardsonian Romanesque architecture and was the masterpiece of famed local architect Arthur Loomis of Clarke & Loomis. Surrounded by a beautiful courtyard neighborhood at the center of the largest collection of Victorian homes in the United States, "Conrad's Castle" featured

Conrad-Caldwell House, 1402 St. James Court. *Courtesy of the author.*

all the latest innovations of the Gilded Age, including interior plumbing and electric lighting. Known for its beautiful woodwork and parquet floor, the Bedford limestone home, covered with gargoyles, beautiful archways and elaborate stone designs, incorporated seven types of hardwoods and magnificent stained-glass windows in its interior design, making the mansion one of the most stunning homes in Old Louisville. The museum has been restored to the Edwardian Age appearance and houses a massive collection of period items, including many original pieces. It stands as a testament to the abundant lifestyle of the owners, two of Louisville's most prominent businessmen and entrepreneurs, Theophile Conrad and William E. Caldwell. The home gives daily tours.[144]

Louisville was also the largest manufacturer of cast-iron gas and water pipes in the United States, under the firm Dennis Long & Company, of the Union Pipe Works, which in 1887 enlarged its capacity by 50 percent. It employed four hundred people with a daily capacity of 250 tons of iron. There were twenty-nine foundries making stoves and architectural and other commercial iron products, employing about four thousand men and consuming about 150,000 tons of coal annually. Louisville ranked fifth among U.S. cities in iron consumption. The city also became a great storage market, with immense supplies stored in warehouses that supplied the nation's demands.[145]

The rolling mill industry made boiler iron, plate and bar. It made steamboat and general steam boilers, railroad car wheels, railroad car and wagon axles, wrought forgings and miscellaneous iron workings. Ainslie, Cochran & Company (Main and Tenth Streets) owned the Louisville Foundry and Machine Shop. A.B. Burnham & Company was a wholesale tinner that made stoves, tinware and plates. It was located on 122–126 Eighth Street. Henry Disston & Sons (250 and 852 West Main Street) made steel tools, saws and files. George Meade, located on the corner of Third and Jefferson, made pig iron. Thomas Mitchell manufactured tanks and boilers.[146]

Louisville had thriving brewing and malting factories employing about five hundred workers with an annual product worth $2,500,000. There were six large breweries in Louisville. The city also made ladies' dresses and men's shirts and fine suits, employing about one thousand tailors and seamstresses. Wanamaker & Brown, located on the northwest corner of Fourth and

Jefferson Streets, made clothing. R. Knott & Sons (557 Fourth Avenue) made dresses and carried fashionable dry goods.

Louisville led the world in farm wagons. It also had a large flour mill that made 1,600 barrels of flour per day. W.H. Edinger & Brothers, located at 133 and 137 East Main Street, was a wholesale flour dealer. A line of manufactured steam bakery goods, including bread, crackers and cakes, was made in the city. The manufacture of confectionary took place in the city. Frank Meene made Eagle Brand chocolates, including 75,000 pounds of candy in 1898. Bradas and Gheens made the Nightingale and Anchor brands of chocolates and was the oldest continuously operated candy factory in the United States. It was the largest chocolate factory in Kentucky.[147]

Louisville was also a leader in making trunks and valises. P.J. Botto & Company, located at 335 Market Street, made trunks and travel bags. Chilton, Guthrie & Company (Twenty-Fourth and Main) manufactured trunks, valises and bags. Shoe manufacturing became one of the most prominent and prosperous trades in the city, reaching its peak in 1886. Theodore Cimiotti & Company (303, 312 and 314 Seventh Street) made men's shoes and boots.

Louisville once led the world as a center of winter pork packing, but when the railroads extended to the West, the industry began to fade. But firms like McFerran, Shallcross and Company were still known for their famous "Magnolia Hams." Refrigeration permitted Louisville packinghouses to work in the summer as well as winter, and the city increased its production to meet the demand of home and regional markets. H.F. Vissman & Company, located at Story Avenue and Buchanan Street, was a pork and beef packer. By the turn of the century, Louisville had the largest livestock market.

In 1887, C.C. Mengel Jr. & Brothers shipped lumber abroad and eventually owned its own fleet of ocean vessels to transport lumber overseas. Louisville also made newspaper and wrapping paper. Three large plants in the city were involved in artificial fertilizers. Paints, colors and varnishes were large and rapidly increasing industries. In addition to millwrighting, copper and brass work, wireworks and tinware were also growing industries. Louisville produced pickles and cider vinegar, chewing gum, patent medicines, plumber's supplies, brooms, stonework, monuments and tombstones, vitrified brick, fire brick and paving materials, terra-cotta and clay sewer pipes, electrical and surgical instruments, steel and wood single trees and neck yokes. These were all thriving industries in Louisville. One thousand people were involved in the publishing, lithographing, binding, electrotyping, stationery manufacturing and paper box businesses.[148] Charles

Dearing was a bookseller whose shop was on the northwest corner of Third and Jefferson Streets. Dupont & Company (226 Sixth Street) made paper, and John Morton Company was a publisher at 440–446 West Main Street. One industry in Louisville that surpassed any other in the world was the manufacture of plows. Four companies made a product valued at $2,275,000 and employed 1,925 workers. B.F. Avery, Thomas Meikle, McCormick Harvest Machine Company and Brinly-Hardy Company all made plows. B.F. Avery, the largest in the world, sent its plows to every country where modern agricultural methods were used. The number of plows made in Louisville in 1880 was 80,000. In 1886, the production increased to 190,000 plows, and the establishment was enlarged in 1887. In 1880, the value of all agricultural implements manufactured in Louisville was $1,220,000 ($27,735,729 in today's currency). By 1887, the value of plows had nearly doubled.[149]

Louisville led the world in hydraulic cement. Most of the cement was made largely from mills operating on the cement stone in the bed of the Ohio River. The cement factories made one million barrels annually. In 1887, the sales for cement reached 850,000 barrels. By the turn of the century, Clark County, Indiana's thirty cement mills made the area one of the nation's leading cement producers. One of the giants in the industry was the Western Cement Company, located on Third and Main Streets in Louisville. The firm's president was R.A. Robinson; James Breckinridge Speed was vice-president. In 1887, the Western Cement Company was the selling agent for all the celebrated brands of Louisville hydraulic cement. In 1829, John Hulme & Company began the manufacture of Louisville cement at Shippingport, which was once located near the foot of the Louisville and Portland Canal. Louisville cement was recognized as the best natural article manufactured in the United States. The Louisville brands comprised the Star, Diamond, Anchor, Acorn and Fern Leaf cements, with two of the mills in Kentucky and six in Indiana. The Louisville brands were praised by engineers and architects around the country. In almost every state or territory west of the Alleghany Mountains where large public works had been constructed, Louisville cement was used either largely or exclusively. It was used for bridges, waterworks, railroad buildings, government improvements on rivers and harbors, customhouses and buildings of every size. Louisville cement was cheap to make with sand, and the cement set properly and hardened regularly and persistently. The cement had the largest aggregate sale of all other cements west of the Allegheny Mountains. It was used for street foundations and was preferred over other cements.[150]

Louisville led the world in tanned sole and harness leather. France took an interest in Louisville's kid leather. There were twenty-two tanneries in Louisville. The value of the annual product was $2,500,000. Nearly eight hundred workers were employed in the industry. Colonel Andrew Cowan made tan leather, as did D. Frantz & Sons, located on the corner of Franklin and Buchanan Streets. George Cross (413 Fourth Avenue) manufactured umbrellas, parasols and kid gloves.[151]

Louisville was the largest market for the sale of mules. The city also manufactured wood and iron. R.B. Cotter, located at 215 Sixth Street, was a dealer in pine and hardwoods. One of the largest veneering mills in the United States moved to Louisville from New York and erected a large building and used forty acres of land and about 500 workers. Enrich & Andriot owned a wagon and buggy manufacturing company and was the largest company in wagon manufacturing in the country. The Bradley Carriage Company (126–128 West Main) made carriages. The furniture manufactories employed 1,200 workers and made a product valued at $1,775,000 annually. The Kentucky Manufacturing Company, owned by J.L. Eschman (Fifteenth Street between Portland Avenue and Duncan Street), made furniture. The Louisville Manufacturing Company (619–621 West Market) made furniture and bedroom suites.[152]

Wholesale druggists also made up a booming industry in Louisville. James Wilder and his brother Edward had one of the largest wholesale druggists in the country. Arthur Peter & Company (716 and 718 West Main Street) also was a wholesale druggist. To meet the refrigeration needs of the meatpacking companies and local consumers, ice companies were established. These included the Talmage Ice Company (505 Third Street) and the Pickett Artificial Ice Company (Floyd between Kentucky and Caldwell Streets). J.W. Reccius & Brother (304 West Market) became the headquarters for baseball supplies and athletic and sporting goods. J.S. Clark & Company (Green Street) made marble and granite; M. Muldoon & Company made monuments; J.M. Clark (122 Second Street) made Hyman's sweet pickles and ketchup; and the Louisville Tent and Awning Company (172 Fourth Avenue) made tents and awnings. Sherman & Company (located on 224 and 236 Sixth Street), Samuel Chambers (located on 230 and 232 West Main Street) and Lewis & Hanford (located on 246 and 248 West Main Street) were wholesalers in seeds. Wholesale grocery was also a profitable business and included J.W. Sawyer (354–356 East Market), Moore, Bremaker & Company (723 and 725 West Main Street), A. Engelhard (213 West Main) and Otter & Company (214, 216, 218, 220 Sixth Street between Main and

Market). Louisville had the largest soap factory in the South and the largest box factory in the world. The city also had the largest exclusive organ factory in the world.[153]

On July 19, 1865, Louisville recorded its first baseball game. Between 1867 and 1870, Louisville played six games with the Cincinnati Baseball Club and the Cincinnati Red Stockings. In 1876, Louisville became a member of the National League. In 1882, the team became a member of the American Association, and the following year, the organization changed its name to the Louisville Baseball Club and established a park at the southwest corner of Twenty-Eighth and Broadway. In 1884, John "Bud" Hillerich made his first baseball bat from white ash. The first bat produced was for Peter Browning, whose nickname was the "Louisville Slugger." The bat became known as the Louisville Slugger. In 1905, Honus Wagner, known as 'the Flying Dutchman," signed a contract as the first player to endorse a bat. In 1911, Frank Bradsby joined J.F. Hillerich, and the company Hillerich & Bradsby & Company became one of the largest manufacturers of baseball bats and other sporting equipment in the world. By 1902, a new baseball park was built at Seventh and Kentucky Streets. Pete Browning became one of the most famous baseball players from Louisville. Today, Hillerich & Bradsby makes one million wooden bats per year. The Louisville Slugger Museum and Factory, located at 800 West Main Street, has the world's largest baseball bat, called the "Big Bat." The current president and CEO of Hillerich & Bradsby is John A. Hillerich IV, the great-grandson of Bud Hillerich. In 2015, Wilson Sporting Goods bought the Louisville Slugger brand from Hillerich & Bradsby. Visitors can tour the factory and purchase the world-famous bat.[154]

On March 27, 1890, a major tornado measuring F4 tore through the Parkland neighborhood to Crescent Hill, destroying 766 buildings and killing between 74 and 120 people. At least 55 people were killed when the Falls City Hall collapsed. It was the highest death toll due to a building collapse from a tornado in U.S. history.

In 1893, two sisters Patty and Mildred Hill wrote the song "Good Morning to All" for their kindergarten students. The lyrics were changed to "Happy Birthday to You."

By the end of the nineteenth century, Louisville's population had increased to 204,000. The new transportation system was changing the form of the urban area. Annexed areas of the city became their own cities, such as Crescent Hill, Clifton, South Louisville and Parkland. Women began to make headway into the workforce. By the end of the nineteenth century,

This page: Louisville Slugger Museum, 800 West Main Street. *Courtesy of the author.*

baseball had emerged as the national sport. The city had a ballpark at Twenty-Eighth and Broadway. The citizens of Louisville also discovered tennis and golf, organizing the Louisville Tennis Club in the 1880s and the Louisville Golf Club in 1893. In 1895, Churchill Downs built the familiar twin spires and a new grandstand.[155]

Filson Historical Society
1310 South Third Street

The Filson Historical Society is located in the Old Louisville neighborhood. Founded in 1884, the organization was named after early Kentucky explorer John Filson, who wrote *The Discovery, Settlement, and Present State of Kentucke* in 1784, which included one of the first maps of the state. The founder and first president of the Filson was Rueben Durrett. The Filson's extensive collections focus on Kentucky, the Upper South and the Ohio River Valley. Its

Filson Historical Society, 1310 South Third Street. *Courtesy of Larry Wright.*

research facilities include a manuscript collection as well as a library that includes rare books, periodicals, maps and other published materials. The headquarters for the Filson is located in the Ferguson Mansion, built in 1905 by the architectural firm Dodd and Cobb. The home is one of the finest examples of Beaux-Arts architecture in Louisville. In 2016, the Filson renovated and constructed the Owsley Brown II History Center.[156]

In 1899, the last gas street lamp was replaced with the light bulb. The foundation laid by the Gilded Age in Louisville would sustain the city into the early 1900s, and businesses continued to thrive. Automobiles, aeroplanes and motion pictures arrived in the city in the early twentieth century. Manufacturing continued to spread beyond Louisville's city limits and entered into Highland Park and Oakdale. The success of the Gilded Age continued into the early twentieth century and could not have been sustained without the foundation work provided by the men who built the city of progress in the 1870s, '80s and '90s.[157]

Chapter 7

WORLD WAR I, PROHIBITION, THE GRAND THEATERS AND THE 1937 FLOOD

1900-1937

On May 1, 1900, Jennie Benedict, along with her partners Salome E. Kerr and Charles Scribner, opened her first store and catering business on 412 South Fourth Street. Several years later, in 1911, she opened a new restaurant at 554 South Fourth Street. She is best remembered for her Benedictine Sandwich spread.[158] In 1902, the Strand Theater, located on 326 West Chestnut Street, opened to the public. The theater was located in the Masonic Temple building. In 1923, the theater installed one of the famous Wurlitzer organs. The theater closed in 1952.

In 1903, the Park Circuit and Realty Company began construction of Fontaine Ferry Park. In 1905, Fontaine Ferry Park opened to the public. The park had four major roller coasters: the Scenic Railway, the Racing Derby, the Velvet Race and the Comet. The park also had Hilarity Hall, where visitors were greeted by the animated laughing Sam and Sue. Hilarity Hall also had the Ever Rolling Barrel, the Sugar Bowl, the Bumpy Slides and the Double Slides. The park also had the famous Gypsy Village and a roller link, swimming pool, bicycle track, penny arcade and hotel.[159]

In 1905, construction began on the Louisville Free Public Library. It opened to the public in 1908. In 1950, the Louisville Free Public Library became the first library in the nation to put its own FM radio station on the air, WFPL. A second station, WFPK, joined WFPL a few years later. Today, the Louisville Free Public Library is the largest public library system in Kentucky.[160]

Above: Fontaine Ferry Park carousel, 1928. *Courtesy of the University of Louisville Digital Archives, Caufield and Shook Collection. https://digital.library.louisville.edu/cdm/singleitem/collection/cs/id/1417/rec/18.*

Left: Fontaine Ferry Park entrance gate, 1949. *Courtesy of the University of Louisville Digital Archives, Caufield and Shook Collection. https://digital.library.louisville.edu/cdm/singleitem/collection/cs/id/7042/rec/2.*

Fontaine Ferry Park, June 1907. *Courtesy of the University of Louisville Digital Archives, Caufield and Shook Collection. https://digital.library.louisville.edu/cdm/singleitem/collection/kyimages/id/10/rec/44.*

Also in 1905, the Western Colored Branch Library opened to the public. It was originally located on 1125 West Chestnut Street. In 1908, Andrew Carnegie donated funds to build a new library building; the Western Colored Branch Library opened in its new location at 604 Tenth Street and became the first library in the nation to serve and be fully operated by African Americans. Today, the Western Branch is home to African American archives, featuring resources dedicated to African American history.[161]

In 1902, the first official Kentucky State Fair was held, and 75,000 people attended the event. In 1907, the annual Kentucky State Fair moved permanently to Louisville. In 1956, the fair moved to the Kentucky Exposition Center.

On April 1, 1907, the Mary Anderson Theater opened to the public as a vaudeville house at 612 South Fourth Street. In the 1920s, the theater switched to movies. The theater was named after the famous actress Mary Anderson, who made her debut in Louisville. The venue closed in the mid-1970s.

This page: The Western Branch of the Louisville Free Public Library. *Courtesy of Steve Wiser.*

On Christmas Day 1908, the Majestic Theatre opened in Louisville. L.J. Dittmar, George Fetter, R.S. Brown, Charles Bohmer and A.P. Barnard organized the Majestic Amusement Company with a capital stock of $15,000. Several buildings at 546–548 Fourth Avenue were torn down to make way for the Majestic. The first house had a seating capacity of 650 people and was at the time the largest in the state and one of the largest in the country. In 1911, the theater expanded its seating capacity to 1,200 patrons. The venue had one of the most elaborate entrances in the country. The interior had black leather seats and wood made of mahogany. In 1912, a special machine was used for Kinemacolor productions. The new building cost $50,000. In 1915, the owners decided to build an even more ornate entrance, one designed along the French Renaissance style. The floor and arch were made from Rookwood and Alhambra tile, the two most expensive tiles produced at the time. The box office was originally made of white marble but later replaced with tile. Louisville at the time was one of the leading exhibiting cities for films.[162] The theater closed in 1928. In 1910, the Waverly Hills Sanatorium opened.

Majestic Theatre at night, Louisville, Kentucky, circa 1922. *Courtesy of the University of Louisville Digital Archives. https:// digital.library.louisville.edu/cdm/ singleitem/collection/cs/id/8757/ rec/4.*

On September 3, 1914, *Louisville Courier-Journal* editor Henry Watterson used the phrase "To Hell with the Hohensollerns and Hapsburgs" and wrote editorials supporting the involvement of the United States in World War I. In 1916, President Woodrow Wilson won the Louisville and Jefferson County votes, in part because of his slogan "He Kept Us Out of the War." In April 1917, the United States went to war. The War Department built Camp Zachary Taylor. The barracks were constructed by 10,000 men and 2,000 carpenters at a cost of $9 million. On September 5, 1917, 28,000 recruits entered Camp Taylor. During the two years of the camp's existence, 150,000 soldiers passed through the gates. By late summer 1918, 44,000 men were being housed in the barracks and another 20,000 in tents. By the time an armistice was signed and the war ended, Louisville had lost 350 soldiers and 3 nurses to the brutal war overseas.[163]

In the fall of 1918, the Spanish flu hit Camp Taylor and the hospital had 13,000 patients. The pandemic claimed 824 soldiers. The city of Louisville was also hard hit. Schools, theaters and churches were closed and large gatherings discouraged. The supply of coffins ran out, and hundreds of cases of the flu developed daily. By October 1918, Louisville had 6,415 cases and Louisville and Jefferson County lost 879 civilians to the flu.[164]

On August 6, 1918, Robert Worth Bingham, the wealthiest man in Kentucky, became the owner of the *Louisville Courier-Journal*.

Camp Zachary Taylor barracks street scene. *Courtesy of the author's collection of postcards.*

Top: Camp Zachary Taylor barracks, general view from the observation tower looking south. *Courtesy of author's collection of postcards.*

Bottom: YMCA Auditorium, Camp Zachary Taylor. *Courtesy of the author's collection of postcards.*

In 1919, A.H. Bowman leased from the federal government fifty acres of property that had been seized by the government and created a wood hangar and opened a field airport. The land originally belonged to the Breckinridge family. Mary Breckinridge married Baron Kurt Von Zedtwitz, and their son Baron Waldemar Konrad Von Zedtwitz inherited the property when both of his parents died. Waldemar Zedtwitz joined the German army. Since the United States was at war with Germany, the United States Alien Property Office seized the property. In 1922, the army took over his lease; in 1923, the field was named Bowman Field. The Louisville Board of Trade purchased Waldemar Zedtwitz's property for $750,000 and a major part of the purchase went toward Seneca Park and the rest went to Bowman Field. In 1928, the Louisville and Jefferson County Air Board was created to administer the airport. On August 1, 1928, Continental Airlines, which later became American Airlines, began carrying mail on the Cincinnati–Louisville link. In 1930, a passenger terminal and paved runways were added to Bowman Field.[165]

After the war, the War Mothers, American Legion and American Legion Auxiliary were formed. At one time, the Jefferson Post was the largest unit of the American Legion in the world. Thousands of soldiers who trained at Camp Zachary Taylor and Camp Knox returned to Louisville, and the city became their town. These men acquired jobs and set up homes and started families. In 1922, Louisville entertained ninety conventions and had an attendance of 200,000 at the Kentucky State Fair. During the 1920s, 192 industries were established in Louisville. Several manufacturing plants were the largest of their kind in the United States, and eighteen were the largest in the South. They produced wagons, hickory handles, reed organs, minnow buckets and baseball bats. Five years after World War I, Louisville had 5,700 mercantile stores, of which 1,200 did wholesale business. The city ranked twenty-second in the value of products manufactured and twenty-fourth in size, having a population of 300,000, with 15 percent of the population being African American. Louisville was the second-largest city in the South, with New Orleans outranking it. Between 1920 and 1925, Louisville's population

Bowman Field, located at 2815 Taylorsville Road. *Courtesy of Steve Wiser.*

increased by 70,000, and 119 new factories were built within two years. In 1911, there were 20,000 passenger cars in Jefferson County; by 1929, that number had increased to 57,000.

Some of Louisville's industries had been around for one hundred years, including Bacons, Stewart Dry Goods, the John P. Morton Company, Kendrick's and Lemon's Jewelry Stores, Peter Neat Richardson Wholesale Drug Company, the B.F. Avery Plow Company, Belknap Hardware (the South's leading wholesale hardware house) and Bradas and Gheens, manufacturers of candy. John Colgan made chewing gum, including Violet Gum Chips and Mint wafers, which included early baseball cards in the tins.[166]

On January 16, 1920, Prohibition went into effect throughout the United States. Early attempts at prohibition had already gone into effect. In 1915, 120 Kentucky counties banned liquor. Louisville had to close twelve breweries and thirty distilleries.[167] The city lost six to eight thousand jobs due to Prohibition.

In 1920, the first zoo was opened at Senning's Park, which currently is Colonial Gardens, next to Iroquois Park. By 1939, the zoo closed due to the effects of the Great Depression. Louisville would not see another zoo until 1969, when the Louisville Zoo opened in the Poplar Level Road neighborhood.

In 1920, Nazareth, which is now Spalding College, opened a college for women.

In 1921, the Rialto opened on Fourth Street. It was Louisville's first movie palace, built at a cost of $1 million. The Rialto was considered the finest theater, with chandeliers made of Bohemian crystal, a grand marble staircase and walls made of Rookwood tiles. The theater closed in 1968.[168] Also in 1921, the Merchants and Manufacturers Building and the State Fairgrounds in the West End opened to the public. In 1956, the Kentucky Fair and Exposition Center replaced it.

On October 6, 1921, the Kentucky Theater opened to the public. Located at 649–651 South Fourth Street, it was operated by the Modern Amusement Company. The building was designed by Joseph & Joseph. In 1940, the theater was remodeled to accommodate seating from 780 to 1,000 patrons and added a balcony. In 1984, the theater became the home of a multimedia slide presentation promoting Kentucky tourism called "The Kentucky Show," which moved to the Old Bardstown Village in Bardstown, Kentucky. The Kentucky Theater closed in 1986. George Stinson bought the theater. In 1998, a nonprofit arts organization called the Kentucky Theater Project Inc. saved the building. The theater served as a community arts center but currently is a restaurant.[169] "The Kentucky Show" also has a long history. After the show closed at the Old Bardstown Village, the show

The Rialto Theatre, Louisville, Kentucky, circa 1947. *Courtesy of the University of Louisville Digital Archives. https://digital.library.louisville.edu/cdm/singleitem/collection/cs/id/6904/rec/5.*

The Kentucky Theater. *Courtesy of Steve Wiser.*

underwent a massive update and was shown at the Kentucky Center for the Arts. According to the Kentucky Science Theater's website, in 2017, "The Kentucky Show" was presented at its location.

In the spring of 1922, WHAS radio came on the air and was a pioneer in the field and one of the first licensed stations in Kentucky. The *Louisville Courier-Journal* and the *Louisville Times* sponsored the radio station. It became one of the largest and most influential radio-casting concerns in the country. During the 1937 flood, WHAS played a leading role in the rescue work.

The Brown Hotel
335 West Broadway

On October 23, 1923, J. Graham Brown, a wealthy businessman, built the Brown Hotel in downtown Louisville at the corner of Fourth and Broadway. That year, Louisville was the thirty-fourth-largest city in the country with a population of 235,000. Fourth Street was already an established promenade, and the Brown Hotel became the cornerstone of the "Magic Corner." The hotel took only ten months to complete at a cost of $4 million. David Lloyd George, former prime minister of Great Britain, became the first person to sign the guest register. The sixteen-story concrete and steel hotel was built in the Georgian Revival style, faced in brick and trimmed in stone and terra-cotta. The interior design of the hotel is primarily of the English Renaissance style, with Adams period detail. In 1923, the Brown Hotel's chef, Fred K. Schimdt, invented the famous Kentucky Hot Brown in the hotel restaurant. The open-faced sandwich was piled high with turkey and bacon, smothered in a mornay cheese sauce and tomato and baked in an oven.[170]

Also in 1922, Isaac Bernheim donated the statue of Abraham Lincoln to the Louisville Free Public Library. In 1925, Hattie Speed, wife of James Breckinridge Speed, donated money for the J.B. Speed Art Museum on the campus of the University of Louisville. The museum cost $800,000. The architect was Arthur Loomis, who used native materials and local workmen. Dr. Preston Pope Satterwhite donated the Gobelin tapestries and the oak-paneled Elizabethan room.

This page: Brown Hotel, 335 West Broadway. *Courtesy of Samantha Del Pozo, CTA. The Brown Hotel, associate director of sales.*

Abraham Lincoln statue, by George Grey Barnard, located at the Louisville Free Public Library, 301 York Street. *Courtesy of the author.*

Speed Art Museum
2035 South Third Street
https://www.speedmuseum.org / 502-634-2700

The Speed Art Museum is Kentucky's oldest and largest art museum. Since 1925, the museum has continued to expand its building and enrich its collection. In 1977, the museum bought Rembrandt's *Portrait of a Woman*. In 2012, the museum closed for a $50 million renovation. In 2016, the Speed Art Museum reopened to the public. The Speed collection spans more than six thousand years of human creativity, culture and experience.

In 1924, the Elks House opened, but in 1928, the building was sold and became the Henry Clay Hotel. On October 5, 1925, J. Graham Brown opened the Brown Theater. Also in 1925, Ford Motor Company opened a new plant at 1400 South Western Parkway, replacing the Third and Eastern Parkway plant. Reed Air Filter became the world leader in design and production of industrial dust control, ventilating and air handling. William Girdler became the only commercial producer of helium. Also in 1925, the University of Louisville moved its School of Arts and Sciences to the Belknap Campus, the former site of the Industrial School of Reform. Enid Yandell was a famous female sculptor who studied in Paris under Rodin and had her American training with Frederick William MacMonnies. She designed the statue of Daniel Boone, which overlooks Cherokee Park.

The Louisville Palace Theater
Fourth Street between Broadway and Chestnut Streets
https://www.louisvillepalace.com / 502-583-4555

On September 1, 1928, the Loew's Theater opened for business. Built by the Austrian American architect John Eberson, who was renowned for his movie houses, this 3,300-seat theater was done in a Baroque style and featured a grand lobby, carvings of more than 140 famous figures from Michelangelo to Eberson himself and a one-thousand-pipe Wurlitzer organ that remained in the theater until 1978. As a first-run movie house located in Louisville's

This page: Speed Art Museum, located at 2035 South Third Street. *Courtesy of Jeff Rawlins.*

entertainment district, Loew's was a symbol of the glitz and glamour of old Hollywood. On its opening in 1928, one could even look up at the dark blue ceiling and see the twinkling stars of lights that were a perfect representation of Eberson's idea of an atmospheric theater. In 1981, the theater's name was changed to the Louisville Palace Theater. It retains the original ticket booth from Loew's Theater, and the building is one of the few theaters by John Eberson still standing. As the only remaining cinema of the grand palace theaters in the city, the Louisville Palace Theater retains the theater's former glory as one of the city's primary venues for entertainment.

W.L. Lyons Brown Theater
315 West Broadway
https://www.kentuckyperformingarts.org/venues/brown-theatre / 502-584-7777

This theater was named after J. Graham Brown. Opened on October 5, 1925, at 315 West Broadway, the neoclassical structure was designed after the Music Box Theater in Manhattan and has a forty-by-forty-foot stage. In the 1930s, the venue was renovated into a movie theater. In the 1960s, it was renovated to accommodate live stage performances. In 1971, it was sold to the Louisville Board of Education and operated under a contract to the Louisville Theatrical Association. The theater was renamed the McCauley Theater, after an earlier Louisville theater located on Walnut Street. In 1982, the theater and adjoining hotel were bought by the Broadway-Brown partnership. In 1997, the Fund for the Arts acquired the building and restored the theater. The Kentucky Center for the Arts manages the theater. The W.L. Lyons Brown Foundation, the Brown family and the Brown-Forman Corporation contributed to the renovation. In 1998, the theater changed its name to the W.L. Lyons Brown Theater, and Owsley Brown Frazier donated money to furnish a main reception area adjoining the Fifth-Third Conference Center, which was named the Frazier Lobby. In 2018, the Kentucky Center Foundation purchased the Brown Theater.[171]

Right: The Louisville Palace Theater, 625 South Fourth Street. *Courtesy of Steve Wiser.*

Below: W.L. Lyons Brown Theater, 315 West Broadway. *Courtesy of Christian Adelberg, vice-president, marketing and communication, Kentucky Performing Arts.*

In 1926, Saint Joseph's Infirmary on Eastern Parkway at Preston Street opened to the public. On September 1, 1928, Loew's Theater opened at a cost of $2.5 million. The theater could seat 3,272 people. In 1950, the theater changed its name to Loew's Palace Theater and, in 1994, changed its name to the Louisville Palace Theater. Also in 1926, the Southern Baptist Seminary on Broadway at Fifth Street opened its new campus. The school taught traditional religious education and missionary training, and the campus built the School of Church Music, the School of Religious Education, the Boyce Bible School, the Carver School of Church Social Work and the Billy Graham School of Missions, Evangelism, and Church Growth. The Southern Baptist Seminary was the world's largest seminary at the time.

In 1928, William Heyburn, president of the Belknap Hardware Company, completed the Heyburn Building, the tallest building in Kentucky at that time. On October 31, 1929, the Second Street Bridge over the Ohio River was erected at a cost of $5 million and operated as the Louisville Municipal Bridge and charged a toll. In 1946, the bonds were paid off and the tolls were removed. On January 17, 1949, the bridge was renamed the George Rogers Clark Memorial Bridge, but most Louisville residents still call it the Second Street Bridge. In 1930, the Masonic Temple was completed.

The Belle of Louisville
https://belleoflouisville.org / 502-574-2992

The steamboat was built in 1914 and designed by James Rees & Sons Company in Pittsburgh, Pennsylvania, and was named the *Idlewild* and served as a ferryboat between Memphis, Tennessee, and West Memphis, Arkansas. In 1931, the *Belle of Louisville* came to Louisville. In 1948, the steamboat's name was changed to the *Avalon*. In 1962, the city of Louisville bought the *Avalon* and the name was changed to the *Belle of Louisville*. In 1988, the *Belle* became the oldest and most authentic river steamboat in the country.

In 1932, the U.S. Post Office, Court House and Custom House were completed. In 1933, the grand experiment of Prohibition ended, and in 1937, Seagrams and Sons opened its new distillery at Seventh Street.

Belle of Louisville, located at the Fourth Street Wharf in Waterfront Park. *Courtesy of the author.*

On December 30, 1933, WAVE went on the air, with its studios atop the Brown Hotel.

In 1937, the Louisville Orchestra was founded by Robert Whitney and Mayor Charles Farnsley. Today, the orchestra is the resident performing group for the Louisville Ballet and the Kentucky Opera. On Black Monday, November 17, 1930, the Great Depression hit Louisville, when the Bank of Kentucky and its holding company, Banco Kentucky, shut its doors, leaving six thousand stockholders penniless. To make matters worse, in January 1937, the Ohio River flooded. On January 19, the river reached flood stage throughout the entire length of the river for 980 miles. By January 21, trolley service was interrupted on major streets. The next day, gas and electric power were restricted and telephone service was discontinued. Railroad service was abandoned, leaving only two trains operating to the north and one to the south. City schools closed. Jewish Hospital was evacuated. By January 24, 1937, 40 percent of residential Louisville was underwater. All light and power failed. WHAS continued to broadcast through Nashville, Indianapolis, Covington and Lexington stations. By January 25, pontoon

Top: Flood scene, aerial view 1937. *Courtesy of the author's postcard collection.*

Bottom: The 1937 flood, Barrett Avenue and Broadway looking north. *Courtesy of the author's postcard collection.*

bridges had been built. The west end of the city was abandoned. By January 27, the flood crest reached its peak and started to recede. Fire engines were placed on rafts and patrolled the waterfronts as precautionary fireboats. The river had reached fifty-four feet above flood stage. Red Cross workers and doctors administered typhoid fever shots to every citizen. Mayor Neville

Miller exhibited excellent ability during the crisis, which won him national recognition. CBS, NBC and the British Broadcast System joined together, tying together five thousand shortwave stations and giving the flood the largest coverage ever established in the history of radio at that time, with all broadcast messages and signals being originally sent from the studios of WHAS. Fifty-four thousand Louisville residents were rescued from floodwaters.[172]

Chapter 8

WORLD WAR II

1940-1948

During World War I, Camp Knox, later Fort Knox, became the birthplace of the Armored Force when mechanization was started by the U.S. Army. All the principal developments in armor were made at Fort Knox, and four armored divisions, consisting of the First, Fifth, Sixth and Eighth, were activated at the base. Hundreds of thousands of tankers were trained at Fort Knox. The army post at the time was one of the largest in the United States. During World War II, Fort Knox contained a regional hospital and various tank battalions and armored centers consisting of fifty thousand men. By 1939, the Seventh Cavalry Brigade had been formed, and in 1931, Major General Daniel Voorhis and Major General Adna R. Chaffee were placed in command of Fort Knox. The First Armored Division and the Armed Force School were organized at Fort Knox. By 1942, Fort Knox had three thousand buildings, and the personnel increased to make the base the fourth-largest city in the state of Kentucky. In 1941, the Army Corps of Engineers built Standiford Field.[173]

Standiford Field
600 Terminal Drive

President E.D. Standiford of the Louisville and Nashville Railroad gave 571 acres near Preston and Audubon Park to the U.S. Army

Corps of Engineers. The corps built the first runway on the property for army aircraft. The federal government turned over the property to the Regional Airport Authority, and all commercial flights began operating from its location. Bowman Field remained open to private planes and operates today as a general aviation facility. On November 25, 1947, Staniford Field opened to passenger flights. American, Eastern and TWA boarded flights at Standiford. On May 25, 1950, Lee Terminal opened at a cost of $1 million. In the 1970s, U.S. Air and Delta began flights out of the airport. In 1985, the terminal was expanded and the airport changed its name to the Louisville International Airport. During the 1980s, the airport expanded two new parallel runaways and doubled its capacity. United Parcel Service located its worldwide hub, called Worldport, to the Louisville International Airport. The Kentucky National Guard's 123rd Airlift Wing operates C-130 transport aircraft from the Air National Guard located at the airport. On January 16, 2019, the Regional Airport Authority changed the name of the Louisville International Airport to Louisville Muhammed Ali International Airport. The facility is currently the second busiest in the United States in terms of cargo traffic and the fourth busiest in the world.[174]

In August 1940, Bowman Field, Louisville's commercial airport, was taken over by the Army Air Corps as a training base. Later, the field was transferred to the Air Transportation Command and after that to the First Troop Carrier Command, which had control until November 1944. On November 1, 1944, Bowman Field came under the jurisdiction of Colonel Walter Storrie as a Personnel Distribution Convalescent Hospital. In April 1945, the headquarters of the AAF Personnel Distribution Command was moved to Louisville. On June 21, 1945, Colonel Benjamin O. Davis, son of an African American army general, was placed in command at Godman Field. Davis took the Ninety-Ninth Fighting Squadron overseas and served with the command in the North African and Italian campaigns. He later saw service with the Twelfth Fighter Command. Under Davis's command, the Fifteenth Air Force completed two hundred missions without losing a single bomber.[175]

Colonel Herbert E. Tomlinson commanded the Louisville Medical Depot, the largest medical depot in the world. The facility employed one thousand people handling medical supplies that were shipped overseas in watertight containers. Nicholas Hospital on the outskirts of the city housed thousands of wounded and convalescing soldiers.[176]

The Jeffersonville Quartermaster Depot, a $1 billion annual enterprise, employed five thousand military and civilian workers. During the Civil War, the depot made shirts and trousers for the Union army. During World War I, twenty thousand seamstresses living in nearby towns turned out almost one million shirts a month, making the Jeffersonville Quartermaster Depot the largest shirt producer in the world. The Jeffersonville Quartermaster Depot produced more than $2,200,000,000 in goods for the war effort.[177]

By 1940, Naval Ordnance was built adjacent to the Louisville and Nashville Railroad Strawberry Yards. Naval Ordnance was built by the federal government but operated by Westinghouse Electric and Manufacturing Company. The U.S. Naval Ordnance Plant contributed to the war effort, making rounds for big guns during the late stages of the war. Many plants and factories in Louisville played an important role during the war. The DuPont Powder Company made smokeless black powder at the Indiana Ordnance works. The Jeffersonville Boat and Machine Company made transport ships for the military. The Curtiss-Wright factory assembled C-46 cargo planes. National Carbide Corporation made calcium carbide and acetylene gas. The Carbide and Carbon Chemicals Corporation and the B.F. Goodrich Synthetic Rubber Plant built a synthetic rubber plant. In 1941, the National Synthetic Rubber Company built a rubber plant. Reynolds Metals and American Air Filter made parts for planes. The Ford Motor plant turned out one hundred thousand military jeeps. Tube Turns and Henry Vogt Machine Company made artillery shell parts. Hillerich & Bradsby made gunstocks.[178]

In 1941, the OHIO Theater opened at 655–657 South Fourth Street. The Art Deco theater had nine hundred seats and was located next to the larger Kentucky Theater. In 1965, the movie theater closed. The façade and marquee, along with the iconic "OHIO" vertical sign, are all that remain of the theater.[179]

On Sunday afternoons at the Rathskeller at the Watterson Hotel, the Colonial Dames organized and ran the Officers Club. Elizabeth Wilson ran the Service Club. In 1944, 65,000 soldiers used the sleeping facilities of the club and more than 96,000 soldiers attended dances.[180]

One of the largest losses to the city was when Major General Simeon Bolivar Buckner Jr., the son of governor and Confederate general Simeon Bolivar Buckner, was killed by the Japanese in June 1945 on Okinawa. Born in Munfordville, Kentucky, he spent much of his youth in Louisville and married into a Louisville family.[181]

In 1946, the Jefferson County Memorial Forest opened to the public. In 1947, International Harvester bought the Curtiss-Wright plant and switched from making airplane parts to making agricultural equipment, automobiles, commercial trucks, lawn and garden products and household equipment. The company would last until 1985. On April 16, 1947, the first gay bar, called the Beaux Arts Cocktail Lounge, opened in Louisville and was located at 604 South Third Street (today, the Henry Clay Hotel) and remained in operation until 1955. In 1948, WAVE-TV began broadcasting. In 1949, the Watterson Expressway opened its first link between Bardstown Road and Breckinridge Lane.

Chapter 9

LOUISVILLE GOES THROUGH TOUGH TIMES: THE STRUGGLE OF EQUALITY AND THE DECLINE OF DOWNTOWN LOUISVILLE

1950-1970

By the 1950s, the city's industrial output and trade had doubled after the war. In 1944, the War Department estimated that eighty thousand people worked in local factories. Standiford Airport, used by the military during the war, was returned to civilian use. Bowman Field also became an integral part of Louisville airline carriers. In the 1950s, highways were built, resulting in Louisville residents moving to the suburbs. This in turn led to a population decline for the city. In 1940, the African American population was 47,200, but by 1950, the population had grown to 57,800. Republican Eugene S. Clayton became the first African American to serve as alderman. In the postwar period, African Americans fought for equality. In 1948, the Louisville Free Public Library opened its facility to African Americans. In 1950, the Kentucky General Assembly repealed the Day Law. The law, passed in 1904, prohibited integration of institutions of higher education. All colleges, including Spalding, Ursuline and Bellarmine, opened their institutions to African Americans. In 1951, the University of Louisville followed the other colleges and allowed African Americans on its campus. The end of the Day Law renewed action for an end to barriers to African Americans. In 1953, Mayor Charles Farnsley ordered that African Americans be allowed into the Iroquois Amphitheater. In 1955, Mayor Andrew Braddus issued an executive order abolishing segregation in all public parks. In 1956, Blacks and Whites attended public schools together. Also during the 1950s, Cassius Clay Jr. began his boxing career. He made his debut on WAVE-TV.

In 1950, Bellarmine College opened and WHAS-11 began broadcasting. In 1951, General Electric built Appliance Park. The Minneapolis-Moline Company bought out B.F. Avery, and Ballard Flour Rolling Mill was merged with Pillsbury Mills. In 1952, the Louisville Ballet, the official state ballet of Kentucky, was founded and is currently one of the most highly regarded regional ballet companies in the country. Also in 1952, the Kentucky Opera Inc. was founded and designated the State Opera of Kentucky in 1982. In 1954, the annual WHAS Crusade for Children telethon began on television. In 1955, Ford Motor Company built a new plant on Grade Lane. In 1956, the Kentucky Fair and Exposition Center opened to the public and became the home of the Kentucky State Fair. In 1956, the Kentucky Derby Festival began as a two-week fair leading up to the Kentucky Derby, which is held the first Saturday in May. The first festivity was the Pegasus Parade. Also in 1956, Freedom Hall opened at the Kentucky Fair and Exposition Center. In 1957, the new interstate highway system opened. In 1957, the St. James Art Show, also called the St. James Art Fair, began in the Old Louisville neighborhood in the St. James-Belgravia Court Historic District. The event is a free public outdoor annual arts-and-crafts show and occurs on the first weekend of October. Today, the show has more than seven hundred vendors and attracts 300,000 people.

During the 1960s and '70s, downtown Louisville began to decline due to suburban growth. In 1960, the Liberty National Bank and Trust built its new bank at 416 West Jefferson. In the summer of 1960, the Carriage House Players performed the very first production of Shakespeare in Central Park. Today, the Kentucky Shakespeare Festival is a nonprofit, professional theater company that presents free to the public productions of Shakespeare plays at the C. Douglass Ramey Amphitheater in Central Park and runs from May through August. The Kentucky Shakespeare Festival is the oldest free, independently operated Shakespeare Festival in North America. In 1963, the 800 Apartments was completed at Fourth and York Streets, which was Louisville's tallest building for almost a decade. In 1965, the Lincoln Income Life Building was completed. In 1967, the Bank of Louisville erected its new building at Fifth and Broadway.

In 1962, the famous Haymarket closed. In 1969, Fontaine Ferry Park, Louisville's most popular amusement park during the early twentieth century, closed. In 1962, the Sherman Minton Bridge was completed, linking Louisville to New Albany. In 1962, the Southeast Christian Church was built and became the largest megachurch in the United States. In 1963, the John F. Kennedy Memorial Brigade opened. In 1964, Actors Theater of

This page: Actors Theater, 316 West Main Street. *Courtesy of the author.*

Louisville was founded. During Halloween, Actors puts on a production of *Dracula*, and during the Christmas holiday season, it puts on a production of Charles Dickens's *A Christmas Carol*. In 1967, the Kentucky Colonels basketball team was founded.

On May 1, 1969, the Louisville Zoological Gardens opened as the "State Zoo of Kentucky." The zoo comprised ninety-eight acres on Trevellian Way between Newburg and Poplar Level. J. Graham Brown donated $1.5 million to the zoo. The zoo is a nonprofit organization dedicated "to the mission to 'Better the Bond Between People and Our Planet' by providing excellent care for animals, a great experience for visitors, and leadership in conservation education." The zoo's collections, which include botanical gardens, are accredited by the Association of Zoos and Aquariums. The Louisville Zoo is also an agency of Louisville Metro Government. The zoo features concessions and catering, multiple playgrounds, several gift shops, rides and attractions, including the Splash Park, Conservation Carousel, Zoo trams, Zoo adventure ropes courses, camel rides and the BOMA African Petting Zoo. Plus, the zoo produces education programs recognized nationwide for excellence and hosts special-event days throughout the year, including Earth Month activities in April, weekend movie nights, holiday events, the 5K Throo the Zoo Run/Walk and the popular "World's Largest Halloween Party!"[182]

In 1973, the Rivercity Mall was completed on Fourth Street between Broadway and Liberty. On April 3, 1974, Louisville experienced an F4 tornado. It tore a path stretching twenty miles and destroyed several hundred homes in the Louisville area and caused extensive damage in Cherokee Park and resulted in two deaths.

With urban renewal in the 1960s and '70s, old landmarks and buildings were torn down, and a preservation movement began with the Old Louisville Association. In 1972, Revered Clyde Crews and Allan Steinberg founded the Louisville Historical League. The league was dedicated to promoting the appreciation and preservation of the cultural heritage and historic environment in the Louisville metropolitan area. Each month, the league visits various locations around the community where history actually occurred, including cemeteries, historic homes and neighborhoods. In 1973, Dr. Harvey Sloane was elected mayor and fought for historic preservation and neighborhood movements. In 1973, the Historic Landmarks and Preservation Districts Commission was founded. In 1978, the Jefferson County Office of Historic Preservation was founded. In 1977, the Commonwealth Convention Center was built. In 1978, the Hyatt Regency was completed.

This page and opposite: Louisville Zoological Gardens, 1100 Trevilian Way. *Courtesy of Steve Wiser.*

In the early 1960s, the weeklong Derby Festival added the Great Steamboat Race, and the festival joined the Louisville Chamber of Commerce. During the 1970s, the Derby Festival developed into a major attraction, adding the Chow Wagon, the Great Balloon Race, the Mini Marathon—which is one of the largest half marathons in the country—bike races and the Run for the Rosé, in which waiters and waitress would run with wine glasses filled with rosé wine; the person with the most wine left at the end of the run was declared the winner. In 1990, the festival added the Thunder over Louisville fireworks display, the largest annual fireworks show in North America and the kickoff for the Derby events. Today, annual attendance for the event exceeds 1.5 million people. Seventy events take place over a two-week period. In 1998, the Kentucky Derby Festival became a private, nonprofit organization that puts on Kentucky's largest annual event. The mission of the Kentucky Derby Festival Foundation is to provide community service that directly contributes to the cultural, educational, charitable and economic development of the community. The foundation perpetuates the festival's impact on the community by developing projects that highlight the festival's influence on the area's cultural heritage. The foundation works to further the festival's educational and charitable mission through exhibitions and performances. It has also provided more than $500,000 in financial support to groups such as Metro United Way's Success by 6, Crusade for Children, Derek Anderson Foundation, Cystic Fibrosis Research, Multiple Sclerosis Society, Music Theatre Louisville, Police Youth Activities League, St. Anthony's Community Center, Nativity Academy at St. Boniface, Alzheimer's Association, Youth Alive, Every1Reads, American Red Cross (tornado relief), Presbyterian Community Center, Plymouth Community Renewal Center and various Kentucky schools. The KDF Foundation established a committee to help oversee the efforts of the thirty-two charitable organizations that utilized the 2014 Derby Festival Marathon and Mini Marathon to raise money for their groups through pledges secured by runners. More than $253,000 was raised for these charities in 2014 alone, with over $2 million having been raised since the program was started in 2005.[183]

In 1975, the Downtowner opened on 105 West Main Street. The popular gay bar was moved to this location after the original bar on 320 Chestnut burned down under mysterious circumstances in 1974. The bar remained open until 1989.[184]

Chapter 10

THE BOURBON CITY: THE REVITALIZATION OF DOWNTOWN AND THE RETURN OF BOURBON IN LOUISVILLE

1980-2020

On February 13, 1981, sewer explosions ripped through the southern part of Old Louisville and near the University of Louisville when chemicals from the Ralston Purina soybean plant leaked into the sewer system and exploded.

In 1983, the Kentucky Center for the Arts opened. The center was created to promote state culture and tourism, provide a home for Louisville's prominent performing arts groups and enable citizens to see international and nationally renowned artists. Caudill, Rowlett & Scott, an architectural firm from Houston, was contracted to design the building with assistance from the Design and Construction Department of Humana Inc. In 1986, the Kentucky Center Governor's School for the Arts was established and, in 1987, celebrated its first class with 120 students attending in six disciplines: creative writing, dance, drama, instrumental music, visual art and vocal music. In 1990, the Kentucky Center initiated the ArtsReach Louisville program, bringing arts involvement and instruction to community centers throughout the city. ArtsReach joined several successful educational programs at the center, such as the Arts Education Showcase, the Kentucky Institutes for Arts in Education and the Arts Academies. All of these programs fulfill the Kentucky Center's mission to bring the arts to every corner of the state. In 1997, the center became the manager of the newly renovated W.L. Lyons Brown Theater on Broadway. The Brown Theater, which is listed in the National Register of Historic Places, currently seats 1,400 patrons in the style and splendor reminiscent of

Louisville's grand past. In 2018, the Kentucky Center Foundation purchased the Brown Theater. The following year, the Kentucky Center opened a new, 2,000-person General Admission or Standing Room Only venue called Old Forester's Paristown Hall.[185]

In 1982, the Auchter Company began construction on the Humana Tower. The twenty-six-story structure, completed in 1985, is known for the pink granite located on its exterior. In 1987, the American Institute of Architects award the Humana Tower the National Honor Award, and *Time* magazine listed the tower as one of the top ten best buildings of the 1980s. The building is the headquarters for Humana Inc., a for-profit American health insurance company. In 2018, Humana was ranked 56 on the *Fortune* 500 list. The company is the third-largest health insurance company in the nation.

In 1987, Garnett purchased the *Louisville Courier-Journal* newspaper. Also in 1987, Kentucky Kingdom amusement park opened at the Kentucky Fair and Exposition Center. In 1988, the Louisville Motor Speedway opened. In 1988, Kentucky Science Center added an IMAX Theater. It is four stories tall. The Kentucky Science Center was previously known as the Louisville Museum of History and Science. That name was changed to the Louisville Science Center, and in 2009, the museum became the Kentucky Science Center. Kentucky's largest hands-on science museum, it is located at 727 West

This page and opposite: Kentucky Center for the Arts, 501 West Main Street. *Courtesy of Christian Adelberg, vice-president, marketing and communication, Kentucky Performing Arts.*

The Louisville Science Center, formerly the building for the Carter Dry Goods and Grocer Company. *Courtesy of the author*.

Main Street, which was part of Whiskey Row. The history of the building dates to 1878, when the building was used as a dry goods warehouse. In 1975, the city purchased the cast-iron façade limestone building, and the science museum moved in. The history of the Kentucky Science Center goes back to 1871, when Louisville opened a museum dedicated to its natural history collection. The museum was renovated in 2014.[186]

In 1988, the headquarters of the Presbyterian Church (USA), the largest Presbyterian denomination, moved to Louisville.

In 1990, the *Louisville Eccentric Observer* was founded. In 1993, the AEGON Center was completed, becoming Louisville's tallest building. From January 17 through January 19, an intense snowstorm brought fifteen inches of snow in a single day, breaking the all-time record of snowfall in one day in the city. Behind the snow was intensely cold air, sending temperatures below zero. Louisville experienced the lowest temperature record of twenty-two degrees below zero.[187]

In 1994, the African American Heritage Foundation (AAHF) was founded with the goal of encouraging the preservation of African American sites,

This page: The Kentucky Center for African American History. *Courtesy of Steve Wiser*.

communities and culture. It began with the preservation of historic structures in the African American community and the recognition of important sites through its historic markers program. The AAHF opened a center located at Eighteenth Street and Muhammed Ali Boulevard. The center is dedicated to showcasing the triumphs in preservation of African American sites. The goal of the Kentucky Center for African American Heritage is to enhance

Roots 101 Museum at the Kentucky Center for African American History. *Courtesy of Steve Wiser.*

This page and opposite bottom: Big Four Bridge, located at 1101 River Road. *Courtesy of Steve Wiser.*

the public's knowledge about the history, heritage and cultural contributions of African Americans in the state. The center also preserves the traditions and accomplishments of the past. The heritage center sits on the historic Louisville Street Railway Complex.[188]

In 1995, Standiford Airport was renamed Louisville International Airport. In 1996, the Louisville Slugger Museum was opened to the public and the Hillerich & Bradsby baseball factory was relocated next to the museum. In 1998, the Southeast Christian Church opened a nine-thousand-seat worship center on Blankenbaker Parkway in Middletown.

In 1999, Phase I of the Louisville Waterfront Park was completed; Phase II was completed in 2004. In 2014, the Big Four Bridge was converted into a bicycle and pedestrian bridge. The six-span railroad truss bridge, crossing the Ohio River connecting Louisville, Kentucky, and Jeffersonville, Indiana, was completed in 1895 and updated in 1929. In 1969, the bridge was taken out of service. The nickname came from the Cleveland, Cincinnati, Chicago, and St. Louis Railway, which was called the "Big Four Railroad." On February 7, 2013, a pedestrian ramp on the Kentucky side of the river was completed, and on May 20, 2014, the Jeffersonville, Indiana ramp was completed. Guests at the Louisville Waterfront Park can walk or pedal across the bridge and visit restaurants such as the Red Yeti or Schimpff's Confectionary.

In 2000, the Louisville Slugger Field opened for the newly renamed Louisville Bats, the minor-league affiliate for the Cincinnati Reds. That same year, the Valhalla Golf Club hosted the PGA Championship (Tiger Woods won the competition). In 2001, the Louisville Bats won the Governor's Cup AAA Championship. In June 2001, Louisville hosted the first Kentuckiana Pride Festival. The event took place on the Belvedere. In 2002, the Louisville Extreme Parks opened. Also that year, the Forecastle Festival began its annual music festival. In 2003, the City of Louisville and Jefferson County merged into a single government. The merger made Louisville the sixteenth- or twenty-seventh-largest city in the United States, depending on how the population is calculated.

In 2004, Fourth Street Live! opened, becoming downtown Louisville's premier dining and entertainment center. The history of Fourth Street Live! dates to the early 1980s, during downtown's revitalization project. The Louisville Galleria was built on the former River City Mall, which opened in 1973. The mall stretched from Liberty to Broadway and was successful at first, but traffic was reintroduced, and the mall was cut back. In 2007, the Louisville Convention and Visitors Bureau opened the new

Louisville Slugger Field, 401 East Main Street. *Courtesy of Steve Wiser.*

Information Center at the north entrance to Fourth Street Live! The visitor center is three thousand square feet and covers bourbon and Colonel Harlan Sanders and Kentucky Fried Chicken. One of the newest attractions at Fourth Street Live! is the Jim Beam Urban Stillhouse. Located on Fifth Street between Muhammed Ali Boulevard and West Liberty Street, the Urban Stillhouse has a small working distillery and bottling line, where guests can learn about bourbon, buy a handcrafted cocktail or pick up merchandise related to Jim Beam. The education experience explores the history of the Beam family.[189]

In 2004, the Frazier International History Museum opened to the public. The museum is located at 829 West Main Street. Founded in 2004 by local philanthropist Owsley Brown Frazier, it was originally called the Frazier Historical Arms Museum. Shortly after opening, the museum expanded its focus to topics of U.S. and world history, with a focus on the state of Kentucky. The Frazier now houses the Stewart Collection, one of the largest collections of toy soldiers and historical miniatures on permanent public display in the world. Subjects of other permanent exhibitions include the Lewis and Clark Expedition, the Civil War and bourbon-whiskey. In 2018,

Fourth Street Live!, located at 411 South Fourth Street. *Courtesy of Steve Wiser.*

the Frazier became the official starting point of the Kentucky Bourbon Trail. Also in 2004, the Kentuckiana Pride Festival hosted its first parade.

On November 19, 2005, the Muhammed Ali Center opened to the public as a nonprofit museum and cultural center in Louisville. The museum is dedicated to boxer Muhammad Ali, a native of Louisville, and is located in the city's West Main District. The six-story, 96,750-square-foot museum cost $80 million to build. The venue includes a 40,000-square-foot, two-level amphitheater and a plaza. The center's three levels of exhibits and galleries explore Muhammad Ali's life and offers visitors the chance to reflect on one's own individual values, inner strength, character and what makes one the greatest person they can be. The museum's interactive and multimedia exhibits explore the six core principles that Muhammad Ali embraced throughout his life and how they gave him the wherewithal to be the best athlete he could be, the strength and courage to stand up for what he believed in and the inspiration to reach people around the world and dedicate himself to helping others.[190]

Also in 2005, the annual Abbey Road on the River was held in Louisville for the first time. The Louisville Cardinals joined the Big East Conference.

Frazier International History Museum, 829 West Main Street. *Courtesy of the author.*

Ali Center, 144 North Sixth Street. *Courtesy of the author.*

The Jim Patterson Stadium opened as the new home of the Louisville Cardinals baseball team.

In 2006, Churchill Downs hosted the annual Breeder's Cup. Also that year, the 21c Museum Hotel opened to the public. The hotel and museum is located on 700 West Main Street in the historic West Main District. The founders of 21c are Laura Lee Brown and Steve Wilson, preservationists and contemporary art collectors. The building comprises five historical warehouses that once housed tobacco and bourbon merchants. One of the structures served as the Falls City Tobacco Bank for several decades in the mid-1800s. The 21c Museum Hotel is currently the flagship establishment of 21c Hotels. The museum hotel has many pieces of contemporary artwork, including a huge remake of Michelangelo's *David*, located just outside its doors. The hotel has ninety-one rooms and combines a contemporary art museum, boutiques and a chef-driven restaurant.[191] In 2007, the University of Louisville opened the LGBT Center. The University of Louisville established the country's first endowed chair in LGBT studies and created an LGBT studies minor. The university also

21c Museum, 700 West Main Street. *Courtesy of the author.*

opened the South's first themed housing community for students interested in LGBT issues and social justice as well as the South's first LGBT-themed study abroad experience.[192]

In July 2007, the Jane Austen Society of North America–Greater Louisville held its first Jane Austen Festival. The festival is held at Locust Grove and features an Austen author, a Regency Emporium, afternoon tea, workshops and a grand ball. It is the largest Jane Austen event in the country.

In 2008, Valhalla Golf Club hosted the biennial Ryder Cup, which was won by the United States. In 2008, Ed Hamilton dedicated his newest statue of Abraham Lincoln at the Lincoln Memorial at Waterfront Park. On February 23, 2008, the Sons of the American Revolution relocated its national headquarters to 803–807 West Main Street in Louisville. The building was formerly home to a variety of tobacco brokers, including the Kentucky Tobacco Company. In October 2010, the SAR Genealogical Research Library opened on West Main Street.

From January 26 through January 28, 2009, a storm brought heavy snow and a catastrophic ice storm to Louisville. Snow totals ranged from four to six inches. The snow fell on top of three-fourths of an inch of ice, causing

Sons of the American Revolution Research Library, located next to the Sons of the American Revolution headquarters. *Courtesy of the author.*

severe damage to trees and power lines. The storm caused Kentucky's largest power outage on record, with 609,000 homes and business without power across the state. In Louisville, 205,000 people were without power for ten days. Sixty-nine schools lost power and closed for a week.[193]

On October 10, 2010, the KFC Yum! Center opened to the public. The multipurpose sports center on Main Street between Second and Third Streets hosts the University of Louisville men's and women's basketball teams, and in 2012, the school's women's volleyball team began using the facility. With 22,090 seats for basketball, the Yum! Center is the largest arena in the United States designed for basketball and the second largest for college basketball. The center has also been used for concerts, including Carrie Underwood, Kenny Chesney, KISS, Metallica, Celine Dion, Phil Collins and Alan Jackson. Also in 2010, Six Flags Kentucky Kingdom closed. Also that year, Churchill Downs hosted the annual Breeder's Cup.

In 2011, the Valhalla Golf Club hosted the annual Senior PGA Championship. Also that year, the Sherman Minton Bridge closed due to cracks found in the main loadbearing structural element, leading to Shermangeddon. Churchill Downs hosted the annual Breeder's Cup.

In 2012, Sherman Minton Bridge reopened. The KFC Yum! Center hosted the 2012 NCAA Men's Basketball Tournament. The following year, the Big Four Bridge reopened as a converted pedestrian walkway from Louisville to Jeffersonville, Indiana, although completion of the walkway would not be completed until 2014. Also in 2013, the Louisville Cardinals won their third men's basketball championship.

In 2014, Kentucky Kingdom reopened as Louisville's theme park. Also that year, Valhalla Golf Club hosted the PGA Championship. The Ohio River Bridges project began construction. The Louisville Cardinals played in their second consecutive College World Series and third overall. The Cardinals also joined the Atlantic Coast Conference.

In 2015, the KFC Yum! Center hosted the second and third rounds of the 2015 NCAA Men's Basketball Tournament. On December 6, 2015, the Abraham Lincoln Bridge was opened for traffic. In 2016, the Speed Art Museum reopened after a three-and-a-half-year renovation costing $60 million. On June 3, 2016, boxing legend Muhammed Ali died and was buried in Cave Hill Cemetery. In November 2015, the National Society of the Sons of the American Revolution unveiled an eight-hundred-pound, eight-foot-high bronze statue of a Minuteman holding a musket on top of quarried Kentucky limestone. The artist was James Muir. The plaque on the back of the monument reads: "Sons of Liberty 1775, To Honor the History

Above: KFC Yum! Center, located at 1 Arena Plaza. *Courtesy of the author.*

Right: *Sons of Liberty* statue, located in front of the Sons of the American Revolution headquarters, 809 West Main Street. *Courtesy of the author.*

Dr. Mark and Cindy Lynn Stadium, 339 Byrne Avenue. *Courtesy of Steve Wiser.*

of Philadelphia Continental Chapter 1901 Pennsylvania Society Founded 1893 By Its Compatriots 2009." On December 18, 2016, the Lewis and Clark Bridge opened in the east end. Louisville City FC began play in the United Soccer League. Louisville quarterback Lamar Jackson became the Cardinals' first Heisman Trophy winner as the top player in college football in 2016.

In 2017, the Louisville Cardinals played in their fourth College World Series. Pitcher and first baseman Brendan McKay was named the consensus college baseball player of 2017. Louisville City FC won the USL Championship.

In 2020, U.S. Lynn Family Stadium opened to the public. The stadium hosts the Louisville City FC soccer team and will become home to Racing Louisville FC of the National Women's Soccer League in 2021. The stadium is located in the Butchertown neighborhood at 350 Adams Street.

NOTES

Chapter 1

1. Johnston, *Memorial History of Louisville*, 36.
2. Ibid., 37.
3. Allison, *City of Louisville*, 3.
4. Johnston, *Memorial History of Louisville*, 38.
5. Casseday, *History of Louisville*, 26.
6. Johnston, *Memorial History of Louisville*, 40.
7. Ibid., 43.

Chapter 2

8. Johnston, *Memorial History of Louisville*, 49.
9. Branden Klayko, "There Used to Be a Fort at Fort Nelson Park: The Complete History of West Main Street's Pocket Park," Broken Sidewalk, February 23, 2015, https://brokensidewalk.com.
10. Johnston, *Memorial History of Louisville*, 50–51.
11. Ibid., 51.
12. Ibid., 52.
13. Ibid.
14. Ibid, 56–57.
15. Ibid., 57.
16. Lewis and Clark in Kentucky, www.lewisandclarkinkentucky.org.

17. Johnston, *Memorial History of Louisville*, 57.
18. Ibid., 262.
19. McMeekin, *Louisville*, 47.
20. Ibid., 48.
21. "John James Audubon," Career Timeline, PBS.org, July 25, 2007.
22. Louisville Audubon Society, www.Louisvilleaudubon.org; McMeekin, *Louisville*, 47.
23. Portland Museum, https://portlandky.org/exhibitions.
24. Kleber, *Encyclopedia of Louisville*, 573–74; Stoneware & Co., "Heritage," https://www.stonewareandco.com.
25. Johnston, *Memorial History of Louisville*, 73.
26. Ibid.
27. Ibid., 364.
28. Locust Grove, https://locustgrove.org.
29. Kleber, *Encyclopedia of Louisville*, 457.
30. Johnston, *Memorial History of Louisville*, 75.
31. Ibid., 68.
32. Leland R. Johnson and Charles E. Parrish, *Triumph at the Falls: The Louisville and Portland Canal* (Louisville, KY: U.S. Army Corps of Engineers, Louisville District, 2007), https://www.lrl.usace.army.mil
33. Johnston, *Memorial History of Louisville*, 79.

Chapter 3

34. McMcMeekin, *Louisville*, 88–89; Yater, *Two Hundred Years*, 34-37.
35. Kleber, *Encyclopedia of Louisville*, 715–16.
36. Johnston, *Memorial History of Louisville*, 80.
37. McMeekin, *Louisville*, 93.
38. Galt House, https://www.galthouse.com.
39. Johnston, *Memorial History of Louisville*, 89.
40. Kentucky Historic Institutions, "U.S. Marine Hospital," https://kyhi.org.

Chapter 4

41. Yater, *Two Hundred Years*, 61.
42. Bush, *Louisville and the Civil War*, 14.
43. Ibid., 14–15.
44. Ibid., 15.
45. Ibid., 16.

46. Ibid., 17.

47. Ibid.

48. Ibid., 17–18.

49. Louisville Water, "Teacher and Classroom Information," https://louisvillewater.com.

50. Bush, *Louisville and the Civil War*, 18.

51. Ibid.

52. Ibid.

53. Messmer, "Louisville on the Eve of the Civil War," 250.

54. Ibid., 250.

55. Zachary Taylor National Cemetery, U.S. Department of Veterans Affairs, National Cemetery Administration.

56. Bush, *Louisville and the Civil War*, 19.

57. Ibid., 19.

58. LouisvilleKy.gov, "History of Metro Hall Building," City of Louisville, https://louisvilleky.gov.

59. Bush, *Louisville and the Civil War*, 21.

60. Yater, *Two Hundred Years*, 67–69.

61. Bush, *Louisville and the Civil War*, 22–25.

62. Ibid., 20.

63. Ibid.

64. Ibid., 21.

65. Ibid.

66. Ibid.

67. Ibid.

68. Ibid.

Chapter 5

69. Messmer, "Louisville on the Eve of Civil War," 286.

70. Van Horne, *Army of the Cumberland*, 2–3.

71. Bush, *Louisville and the Civil War*, 30–31.

72. Ibid., 31.

73. Beach, *Civil War Battles, Skirmishes*, 16–17.

74. Ibid., 18.

75. Bush, *Louisville and the Civil War*, 38.

76. Ibid.

77. Ibid., 56.

78. "The Murder of General Nelson," *Harper's Weekly*, October 18, 1862.

79. Bush, *Louisville and the Civil War*, 75.
80. Magruder, *Three Years in the Saddle*, 1865.
81. Ibid., 44.
82. Ibid., 49–50.
83. Messmer, "Louisville on the Eve of Civil War," 220–21.
84. Ibid., 227.
85. Beach, *Civil War Battles, Skirmishes*, 154–56.
86. Ibid., 177.
87. Ibid., 198, 201, 202.
88. Ibid., 202.
89. Vest, "Was She or Wasn't He?," 25–26, 42.
90. Ibid.
91. Beach, *Civil War Battles, Skirmishes*, 228.

Chapter 6

92. Ibid., 13.
93. Marianne Zickuhr, "The Brennan House," Explore Kentucky History, https://explorekyhistory.ky.gov.
94. Bush, *Men Who Built Louisville*, 14.
95. Thomas Edison House, http://www.edisonhouse.org.
96. Bush, *Men Who Built Louisville*, 14–15.
97. Ibid., 15.
98. Historic Louisville Guide, "Union Station," http://historiclouisville.com.
99. Bush, *Men Who Built Louisville*, 15.
100. Ibid.
101. Ibid.
102. Ibid., 16.
103. Ibid., 39.
104. Ibid., 16.
105. Ibid.
106. Yater, *Two Hundred Years*, 98.
107. Bush, *Men Who Built Louisville*, 17.
108. Yater, *Two Hundred Years*, 97.
109. Allison, *City of Louisville*, 21.
110. Bush, *Men Who Built Louisville*, 18.
111. Ibid.

112. Churchill Downs, "The History of Churchill Downs," https://www.churchilldowns.com.
113. Bush, *Men Who Built Louisville*, 18.
114. Ibid., 19.
115. Kleber, *Encyclopedia of Louisville*, 822–23; "Simmons History," Simmons College of Kentucky, https://www.simmonscollegeky.edu.
116. Elstner, *Industries of Louisville*, 24.
117. Bush, *Men Who Built Louisville*, 19.
118. Ibid., 20.
119. Elstner, *Industries of Louisville*, 39.
120. Allison, *City of Louisville*, 20.
121. Bush, *Men Who Built Louisville*, 20.
122. Company-Histories.com, "Companies by Letter: American Printing House for the Blind," https://www.company-histories.com.
123. Bush, *Men Who Built Louisville*, 20.
124. The Seelbach Hilton Louisville, "The Seelbach Experience," http://www.seelbachhilton.com.
125. Bush, *Men Who Built Louisville*, 21.
126. Johnston, *Memorial History of Louisville*, 261.
127. Ibid., 261.
128. Bush, *Men Who Built Louisville*, 22.
129. Johnston, *Memorial History of Louisville*, 262.
130. Huckelbridge, *Bourbon*, 64.
131. Ibid., 118.
132. Ibid., 119.
133. Ibid., 122.
134. Ibid., 126.
135. Allison, *City of Louisville*, 16.
136. *Louisville: Nineteen Hundred and Five*, 18.
137. Bush, *Men Who Built Louisville*, 24–25.
138. Whiskey Row, "History of Whiskey Row,' https://kadwebsite.wixsite.com.
139. Thomas Watkins, "The Tobacco Trade of Louisville," in Johnston, *Memorial History of Louisville*, 251.
140. Bush, *Men Who Built Louisville*, 28.
141. Watkins, "Tobacco Trade of Louisville," 256.
142. Ibid., 259.
143. Allison, *City of Louisville*, 17.
144. https://conrad-caldwell.org/brief-history.

145. Allison, *City of Louisville*, 17.
146. Bush, *Men Who Built Louisville*, 30.
147. Ibid., 30.
148. Johnston, *Memorial History of Louisville*, 280–81.
149. Bush, *Men Who Built Louisville*, 32.
150. Allison, *City of Louisville*, 95.
151. Bush, *Men Who Built Louisville*, 32.
152. Ibid.
153. Ibid., 32–33.
154. Louisville Slugger Museum & Factory, www.sluggermuseum.com; Kleber, *Encyclopedia of Louisville*, 387–88.
155. Bush, *Men Who Built Louisville*, 33.
156. The Filson Historical Society, "History," https://filsonhistorical.org.
157. Bush, *Men Who Built Louisville*, 33.

Chapter 7

158. Falk, *Louisville Remembered*, 27–29.
159. Fountaine Ferry Park website, http://www.fontaineferrypark.com.
160. Louisville Free Public Library, "LFPL: A History of Pride and Resourcefulness," LFPL.org, https://www.lfpl.org.
161. Louisville Free Public Library, "Western Library," https://www.lfpl.org.
162. "Majestic Theater," *Moving Picture World* 27 (March 4, 1916): 1461.
163. Yater, *Two Hundred Years*, 168.
164. Ibid., 169.
165. Ibid., 178.
166. McMeekin, *Louisville*, 231.
167. Yater, *Two Hundred Years*, 173.
168. "The Rialto," OldLouisville.com, http://oldlouisville.com/Ruins/Rialto/Rialtoruins.htm.
169. Cinema Treasures, "Strand Theater," http://cinematreasures.org/theaters/30244.
170. The Brown Hotel Louisville, https://www.brownhotel.com.
171. Brown Theatre, "Brown Theatre: History," https://www.kentuckyperformingarts.org.
172. McMeekin, *Louisville*, 241–46.

Chapter 8

173. McMeekin, *Louisville*, 250.
174. Louisville Muhammad Ali International Airport, "SDF History," FlyLouisville.com, https://www.flylouisville.com.
175. McMeekin, *Louisville*, 251.
176. Ibid, 252.
177. Ibid., 252–54.
178. Ibid., 254; Yater, *Two Hundred Years*, 208–9.
179. Cinema Treasures, "Ohio Theatre," http://cinematreasures.org.
180. McMeekin, *Louisville*, 254.
181. Ibid.

Chapter 9

182. The Zoo Louisville, "About the Zoo," LouisvilleZoo.org, https://louisvillezoo.org.
183. Kentucky Derby Festival Foundation, https://discover.kdf.org.
184. Andrew Henderson, "LGBT History 'Reclaimed' in Historic Louisville Properties," *Courier Journal*, June 30, 2017, https://www.courier-journal.com.

Chapter 10

185. Brown Theatre, "History," https://www.kentuckyperformingarts.org.
186. Kentucky Science Center, "History & Impact," https://kysciencecenter.org/about/history-and-impact.
187. "Top Ten Winter Weather Events in Southern Indiana and Central Kentucky," National Weather Service, weather.gov.
188. Kentucky Center for African American Heritage, "About the Kentucky Center for African American Heritage (KCAAH)," https://kcaah.org.
189. Fourth Street Live!, https://www.4thstlive.com.
190. Ali Center, https://alicenter.org.
191. 21C Museum Hotel Louisville, https://www.historichotels.org/us/hotels-resorts/21c-museum-hotel-louisville-by-mgallery/; 21C Museum Hotels, https://www.21cmuseumhotels.com/company/about.

192. University of Louisville, "The LGBT Center at University of Louisville: Our History," LGBT Center at University of Louisville, https://louisville.edu.
193. "10 Years Later: Remembering the 2009 Ice Storm," January 26, 2019, WDRB.com.

BIBLIOGRAPHY

Books

Allison, Young Ewing. *The City of Louisville and a Glimpse of Kentucky*. Louisville, KY: Published under the direction of the Committee of Industrial and Commercial Improvement of the Louisville Board of Trade, 1887.

Beach, Damien, *Civil War Battles, Skirmishes, and Events in Kentucky*. Louisville, KY: Different Drummer Books, 1995.

Bush, Bryan, *Louisville and the Civil War: A History and Guide*. Charleston, SC: The History Press, 2008.

———. *The Men Who Built Louisville: The City of Progress in the Gilded Age*. Charleston, SC: The History Press, 2019.

Casseday, Ben. *The History of Louisville, from the Earliest Settlement till the Year 1852*. Louisville, KY: Hull and Brother, 1852.

Elstner, Charles. *The Industries of Louisville, Kentucky, and of New Albany, Indiana: Their Natural, Mercantile, Manufacturing, Financial and Commercial Resources and Facilities*. Louisville, KY: J.M. Elstner & Company, 1886.

Falk, Gary. *Louisville Remembered*. Charleston, SC: The History Press, 2009.

Huckelbridge, Dane. *Bourbon: A History of the American Spirit*. New York: William Morrow, HarperCollins Publishers, 2014.

Johnston, J. Stoddard. *Memorial History of Louisville from Its First Settlement to the Year 1886*. Louisville, KY, 1887.

Kleber, John, ed. *The Encyclopedia of Louisville*. Lexington: University Press of Kentucky, 2001.

Louisville: Nineteen Hundred and Five. Louisville, KY: Commercial Club, 1905.

Magruder, Henry. *Three Years in the Saddle: The Life and Confession of Henry Magruder. The Original Sue Munday, the Scourge of Kentucky.* Louisville, KY: published by his captor Maj. Cyrus J. Wilson, 1865.

McMeekin, Isabel McLennan. *Louisville: The Gateway City.* New York: Julian Messner Inc., 1946.

Thomas, Samuel, ed. *Cave Hill Cemetery: A Pictorial Guide and Its History.* Louisville, KY: Cave Hill Cemetery Company, 1985.

————. *Louisville Since the Twenties: A Sequel to Views of Louisville Since 1766.* Louisville, KY: Courier-Journal and Louisville Times, 1978.

————. *Views of Louisville Since 1766.* Louisville, KY: Courier-Journal and Louisville Times, 1971.

Van Horne, Thomas. *The Army of the Cumberland.* New York: Smithmark Publishers, 1996; original printing, 1875.

Wood, F.E. *The Louisville Story: A Report of the Sinking Fund Commission of Louisville.* Louisville, KY, 1951.

Yater, George. *Two Hundred Years at the Falls of the Ohio: A History of Louisville and Jefferson County.* Louisville, KY: Heritage Corporation, 1979.

Articles and Newspapers

Messmer, Charles. "Louisville on the Eve of Civil War." *Filson Club History Quarterly* 50, issue 3 (July 1976): 286.

"The Murder of General Nelson." *Harper's Weekly*, October 18, 1862.

Vest, Stephen M. "Was She or Wasn't He?," *Kentucky Living*, November 1995.

Websites

American Printing House of the Blind. https://www.company-histories.com/American-Printing-House-for-the-Blind-Company-History.html.

Brown Hotel. https://www.brownhotel.com.

Churchill Downs. https://www.churchilldowns.com.

Conrad-Caldwell House. https://conrad-caldwell.org.

Filson Historical Society. https://filsonhistorical.org.

Fontaine Ferry Park. http://www.fontaineferrypark.com.

Fort Nelson Park. https://brokensidewalk.com/2015/fort-nelson-park-history.

Galt House. https://www.galthouse.com/boutique-hotel-louisville-ky.

Kentucky Center for African American Heritage. https://kcaah.org/about.

Kentucky Derby Festival Foundation. https://discover.kdf.org/the-foundation.

Kentucky Historical Society Markers, Explore Kentucky. https://explorekyhistory.ky.gov.

Kentucky Performing Arts. https://www.kentuckyperformingarts.org.

Lewis and Clark Expedition in Louisville. www.lewisandclarkinKentucky.org.

Locust Grove. https://locustgrove.org.

Louisville Audubon Society. www.Louisvilleaudubon.org.

Louisville Muhammed Ali International Airport. https://www.flylouisville.com.

Louisville Slugger Museum and Factory. www.sluggermuseum.com.

Louisville United States Marine Hospital. https://kyhi.org/u-s-marine-hospital.

Louisville Zoo. https://louisvillezoo.org.

National Weather Service. weather.gov.

PBS.org. "John James Audubon, Career Timeline." www.pbs.org/johnjamesaudubon. July 25, 2007.

Portland Museum. https://portlandky.org.

Simmons College. https://www.simmonscollegeky.edu.

Thomas Edison House. http://www.edisonhouse.org.

21c Museum and Hotel. https://www.21cmuseumhotels.com/company/about.

Union Station. http://historiclouisville.com/union-station.

University of Louisville, https://louisville.edu.

WDRB.com. www.WDRB.com.

Western Branch of the Louisville Free Public Library. https://www.lfpl.org/branches/western.htm.

Whiskey Row. https://kadwebsite.wixsite.com/whiskey-row.

INDEX

ABOUT THE AUTHOR

B ryan Bush was born in 1966 in Louisville, Kentucky, and has been a native of that city ever since. He graduated with honors from Murray State University with a degree in history and psychology and received his master's degree from the University of Louisville in 2005. Bryan has always had a passion for history, especially the Civil War. He has been a member of many different Civil War historical preservation societies and roundtables. He has consulted for movie companies and other authors, coordinated with other museums on displays of various articles and artifacts, has written for magazines such as *Kentucky Civil War Magazine*, *North/South Trader*, *The Kentucky Civil War Bugle*, the *Kentucky Explorer* and *Back Home in Kentucky* and has worked for many different historical sites. In 1999, Bryan published his first work, *The Civil War Battles of the Western Theater*. Since then, he has published over fourteen books on the Civil War and Louisville history, including several titles for The History Press, including *Louisville and the Civil War: A History and Guide* and *Louisville's Southern Exposition, Favorite Sons of Civil War Kentucky* and *The Men Who Built the City of Progress: Louisville during the Gilded Age*. Bryan Bush has been a Civil War re-enactor for fifteen years, portraying an artillerist. For five years, Bryan was on the board of directors and served as a curator for the Old Bardstown Civil War Museum and Village: The Battles of the Western Theater Museum in Bardstown, Kentucky, was a board member for the Louisville Historical League and was the official Civil War tour guide for Cave Hill Cemetery. In December 2019, Bryan Bush became the park manager for the Perryville State Historic Site.